BAD*MANNERS
BRAVE NEW MEAL

RODALE

Copyright © 2021 by Bad Manners LLC

All rights reserved.
Published in the United States by Rodale Books, an imprint of Random House, a division of Penguin Random House LLC, New York.
rodalebooks.com

RODALE and the Plant colophon are registered trademarks of Penguin Random House LLC.

Library of Congress Cataloging-in-Publication Data is available.

ISBN 978-0-593-13510-5
Ebook ISBN 978-0-593-13511-2

Printed in the United States of America

Photographer: Matt Holloway
Recipes: Michelle Davis
Cover designer and illustrator: Nick Hensley
Editor: Dervla Kelly
Art director: Marysarah Quinn
Designer: Kara Plikaitis
Production editor: Mark McCauslin
Production manager: Kelli Tokos
Compositors: Merri Ann Morrell and Hannah Hunt
Indexer: Elizabeth T. Parson

1st Printing

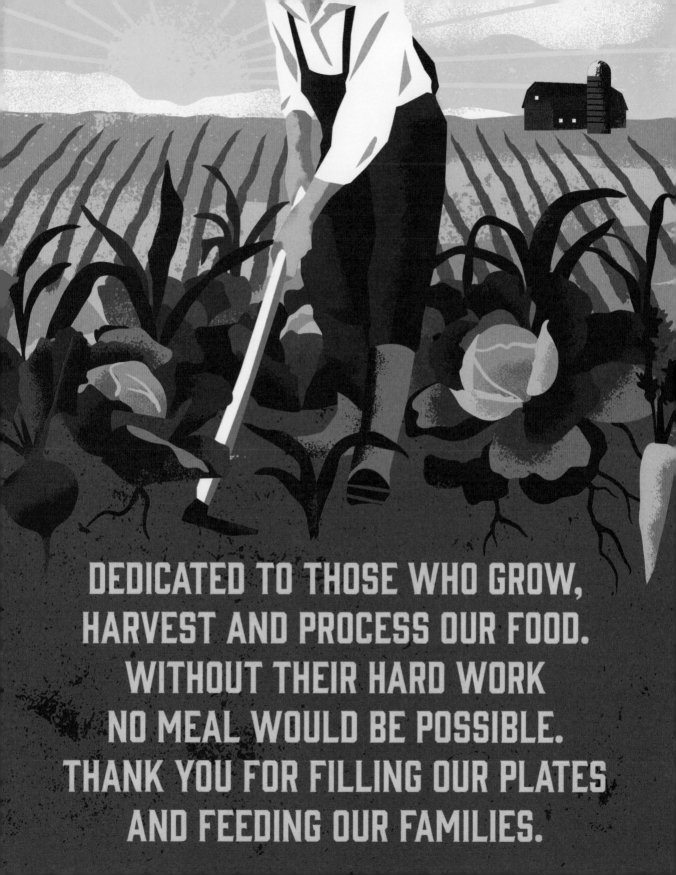

DEDICATED TO THOSE WHO GROW,
HARVEST AND PROCESS OUR FOOD.
WITHOUT THEIR HARD WORK
NO MEAL WOULD BE POSSIBLE.
THANK YOU FOR FILLING OUR PLATES
AND FEEDING OUR FAMILIES.

INTRODUCTION: WHAT THE FUCK HAPPENED? 8

18 BREAKING BED: BREAKFAST

44 CRAVEABLE CORNERSTONES:
SOUPS & SALADS

64 AFTERNOON APPETITE:
SNACKS & SIDES

98 FEAST DE RESISTANCE:
MAIN DISHES

146 TWILIGHT TREATS:
DESSERTS & DRINKS

KITCHEN CREDO: EVERYDAY STAPLES 176
GARDEN OF EATIN: PRODUCE GLOSSARY 216
ICON INDEX 250
RECIPE INDEX 252
ACKNOWLEDGMENTS 256

Not that long ago every social media platform was littered with poorly lit food photos captioned with enough hashtags to induce a headache. There was always another video with some rainbow-colored dish that nobody would ever eat. Delivery apps and takeout had reached a fever pitch, bringing the drive-thru into our driveways, all while exploiting restaurants and delivery workers. We decided it was somehow faster to wait an hour for food to get delivered by underpaid, overworked drivers than to make it ourselves in the same amount of time. We mindlessly threw away our money and health with all those takeout bags and plastic forks we got by the fistful. We worked 60- to 80-hour weeks just scraping by, while reassuring ourselves that we loved the hustle.

THE FUCK?

Ya know, the "rise and grind" bullshit. We ate what we could get, when we could get it, only looking to be full not fed. We were redlining our diet as much as our lives to reach a goal that none of us were totally clear on. We thought the rise of self-care meant that we should spoil ourselves, instead of cutting out the crap that was stressin us out in the first place.

Food culture had devolved into only a couple of ways to eat: conspicuously consuming healthy or trendy food so that everybody could see how cool, disciplined, or dedicated you were; or shoveling whatever you could find into your mouth when you finally realized you hadn't eaten in twelve hours. Most of us were living like this, in one form or another, and nobody seemed to even notice.

We all sat on our asses while our relationship with food spoiled.

Maybe you were in the first camp. You let your "camera eat first" then picked at the plate of trendy food in front of you. You showed off your avocado toast, your cronut, and your ramen burger knowing damn well that you were only gonna have a green juice during the day and some buttered noodles at night. You cosplayed as someone who liked food, but really you liked getting attention for having good taste and enough disposable income to always be eating out. We've met tons of people like this. They start demanding food for free in exchange for "exposure" for the restaurant. They act like they're somehow creative, somehow helping, when all they're really doing is wasting food, not giving honest reviews, and making the rest of us feel broke. That shit is performative and certainly no way to live, let alone eat.

Maybe that wasn't you though. Maybe you were the disciplined, social media-savvy self-appointed Healthiest Person in the Room™. You were always primed to talk about a new powder, an exotic mushroom, or cleanse that was changing your life, which, yeah, you said was perfect last month but now it's like, extra perfect. It was keto, celery juice, paleo, or some other kind of pseudo-science restriction that was repackaged by you as some holy nourishment. We've met so many wellness influencers like this who charge hundreds of dollars so you could watch them make matcha lattes. When that doesn't get them enough attention they quietly distance themselves from orthorexic narratives they pushed on their audience last year and rebrand with the hottest new advice. Now they promised they were advocating for something way better. They were gonna cleanse you of all the toxins, heavy metals, and parasites they were certain you had. You weren't perfect, not like them. You just needed to give them your money, click the affiliate links, and realize there is no greater pleasure than feeling superior to everyone else, particularly when it comes to food. These kinds of people swear that their obsession with cleanliness, perfection, or finding a cheat code to health is the same thing as having a healthy connection with food.

Naw, babe, the only toxin you need to get out of your system is your toxic-ass relationship with food.

The rest of us were watching from the sidelines and thought that we couldn't care THAT much about our diets, so we might as well not care at all. Sure, we'd order a side salad once in a while or give up sugar for a weekend or whatever we thought might count as "healthy." But we didn't mean it. Not really. We ate in our cars while talking on the phone; defrosted some cafeteria-style dinner we'd watch slowly dance around the microwave late at night; or we'd hit

the drive-thru every day because any minute not spent working was a minute wasted. We shoveled bite after bite into our mouths so fast that we forgot what good food tasted like. We forgot we're supposed to nourish ourselves, not just fill our bellies so we can move on to the next fucking hoop we hafta jump through. We were conned by convenience, and our relationship with food and our own bodies suffered. We're just as guilty as the dumb fucks selling us snake oil or pictures of food they didn't cook and never ate. One way or another, everyone felt fucking terrible, and breaking the cycle felt impossible.

Then, almost overnight, all that shit changed. The world stopped just long enough for all of us to get a glimpse behind the curtain. When work stopped or slowed, we all spent more time at home. Lots of us realized that we all worked so fucking hard that, with our punishing schedule gone, we had no lives. Our homes were just places we slept. We didn't know how to fill the hours of the day because we hadn't even had an hour alone with our thoughts in years. Finally at this slowed-down speed we could see all the cracks and breaks in our society that we'd been hustling too fast to see. Our world was deeply fucked up before the global pandemic, but it took the murky, unprecedented halt of so much of our daily lives for us to see that we shouldn't fucking live like this.

Reassuringly, in 2020 many of us felt a tug toward a better tomorrow. Our brains went into caveman-mode and

instinctually we had to start thinking about self-reliance, not self-aggrandizement. We all got back in the kitchen, some of us reluctantly, and our relationship with food was forced to evolve. Flour got scarce as we reconnected with baking. Collectively we remembered we don't need to be so dependent on other people to feed ourselves. We realized that if we can commute an hour to work, juggle a dozen different schedules, remember everyone's coffee order, and be on time to all the meetings then surely we could bake a fucking loaf of bread while in our pjs. We're capable as hell. We've always known what we should be doing, but we were lulled into thinking about food as either a chore or a novelty. When you're stuck at home for days, weeks at time, things come into sharp relief. When the world seems uncertain you hafta sit down and ask yourself, "what the fuck actually matters?" People overwhelmingly moved toward home-cooked meals and patio gardens. We've seen the largest spike in people growing their own food in the United States since the Second World War. And it's about goddamn time, as a normal trip to the grocery store has become the world's shittiest scavenger hunt. Even as authors of three previous cookbooks we had to sit down and wonder how the fuck we wanted to be eating in this new world. Was it finally okay for meals to take longer to make if the payoff was amazing? Can something feel elevated but not be too intimidating to cook? Are people ready to really learn instead of just following directions? So, no, this was not the cookbook we had originally

written. But that's a good thing. The world changed and we decided to write the book we need now, not some book conceived in the "before times." When shit catches fire sometimes you just gotta throw your plans into the flames and warm yourself by the embers. It's called growth.

A food reckoning is unfolding in front of us. Adjustments are difficult and change is scary, but this is an opportunity. A chance for food not just to be different, but better. No more performance art about the perfect diet. No more over-the-top dishes that are intentionally obscene. And no more celebrating entitled, petulant chefs while ignoring home cooks and how average folks eat. Despite whatever chaos is happening outside your door right now, a few things remain true:

1. You're still here. Look at you. You're a living, breathing, sexy-ass motherfucker. You're capable. Shit, you're more than capable—you're intelligent. Your purchase of this cookbook clearly shows just how smart you are.

2. Food still tastes amazing. None of us ever stopped loving food, but we sure as shit took it for granted. We trusted faceless food manufacturers to nourish us while they focused on protecting shareholders and lobbying for subsidies. But that's not food's fault. Food is our truest love and we just took the long way to the altar.

3. Eating a meal you cooked yourself is delicious but also empowering as fuck. Sure, there's a lotta unseen work beyond just warming up some ingredients. You hafta plan, shop, prep, cook, and clean. And yeah, all that shit can be time-consuming, but it's cheaper than ordering delivery, it's healthier when you control what you put into your food, and it's an act of true self-care. Start thinking of cooking like doing laundry or bathing. You can put it off for only so long before you start feeling pretty gross. Cooking is self-reliance. Independence. Cooking is motherfucking freedom. You like being free, right? Fuck yeah you do. Smart people love freedom and we've already established your intelligence in point number one.

4. Cooking is universally attractive.
This isn't stressed enough. Nobody's ever gone on a date and afterward debriefed with a friend like, "Sure they're funny, employed, museum-worthy body, buuuut… they cook." Ya don't exercise? Learn to cook. Drive a shitty car? Learn to cook. Don't have dental insurance? Uncontrollable sweat glands? Look, there's a lot that people are willing to overlook if you can whip up a tasty and nutritious meal. We want you to get laid as much as you want you to get laid.

Even if a few dishes are all you got under your belt, then goddamn it, cook the absolute hell out of 'em. Make your friends and family beg for the recipes. Your roommates should feel compelled to post Yelp reviews when you serve up supper. You should be planning your next culinary challenge as soon as you sit down to eat the one you just conquered. And that's where we come in.

Cooking for yourself doesn't mean you're relegated to instant noodles, subpar sandwiches, and bagged salads. We know you better than that. You're not

stupid, and even the most basic bodegas have enough ingredients for you to turn out some world-class meals with a little guidance from us. Not to mention, when you get your skills dialed in you get to make each meal exactly to your taste. No more picking around foods that you don't like. No more hoping they saw your 'no tomatoes' note on your delivery. It's your dinner exactly how the fuck you want it. Every. Single. Time.

The more you cook, the more you're able to improvise, subbing in and out ingredients based on what you have and still turn out a dope dinner. That's when cooking turns from a chore to art and it feels natural as fuck. But you hafta stick with it. Nothing worth learning was ever learned overnight, but you're already halfway there with this book. You like to eat and you kinda know what you like. Now you just gotta figure out how to do that shit at home, and we're here to help you do everything but the cleanup. Also, cooking for yourself means you learn way more about all the food you've already been eating. There's enough uncertainty in this world without having to guess what the fuck is in baba ghanoush or if peanut butter has dairy in it. Cook for yourself and you'll learn more about food, the world, and your taste. Look at all that motherfuckin growth.

Did you look at the front cover of this book and wonder what half the shit was on there? We get it.

Most people are used to buying food to assemble at home (canned soup, boxed mac and cheese, veggies in microwavable bags) and think that's cooking. But it's fucking not. You need to start buying ingredients, not products. And there's no better place for you to start this journey than the produce section of your grocery store or local market. If you're intimidated by fresh fruits and veggies, you're not alone. That's why the produce section stayed fully stocked while everyone else was fighting over the last burrito in the frozen aisle. It's time you step up. EMBRACE CHANGE, IT'S DELICIOUS.

Plus, the world has gotten so full of shit lately that you could definitely use the fiber. We all could. Study after study confirms that eating lots of fiber from vegetables, fruits, and whole grains can decrease your risk of dying from both heart disease and cancer. An analysis of more than 250 studies shows that people who ate the most fiber reduced their risk of dying from cardiac disease, stroke, type 2 diabetes, and colon cancer by 16-24% compared with stubborn motherfuckers who ate little to no fiber. Reaching for an apple yet? Studies have also shown that dietary fiber intake is associated with a decreased risk of death. FROM. ANY. CAUSE. Those eating the highest amount of fiber reduced their risk of dying by 23% compared with those eating the least amount of fiber. No crazy weightlifting, no running, no weird smoothie cleanse—just eating real foods, rich in fiber, can reduce your risk of death by almost one quarter. So why not take this shit more seriously?

We know you're ready for this new food journey and we're excited to be your sous chef. Hell, we've already written three bestselling cookbooks so we KINDA know what we're doing. Let us help. The kitchen is your science lab as much as it's your place to feel some fucking joy when a recipe comes together into a meal. Try tuning out whatever mushroom cloud of chaos is happening outside your front door. Global pandemics, biblical plagues, the return of low-rise jeans—none of that shit matters in here. We'll help you do more than just survive all these changes. You're gonna thrive, bitch. The new normal is homecooked meals, a full freezer, and eating out just to inspire you cooking more new shit at home. You're gonna feel better about yourself, love your nourished body, and really appreciate all that extra money in your wallet. We'll show you the way.

Systematic change can often feel overwhelming, but let's start small, in our own kitchens. First, we've got to cook what we've got and stop wasting so much goddamn food. Sure, food waste happens everywhere in the food system, from grocery stores to restaurants, but we're fully fucking up at home too.

It's estimated that 43% of all food waste in the United States occurs at home.

We toss 27 million tons of good food THAT WE BOUGHT each year. That means that Americans are spending $144 billion dollars every year for food they never eat and just throw in the trash. Not only is this a waste of resources and labor, but it's spitting in the face of every single person and child facing food insecurity in our communities.

We can be better. Now is that time.

Eating for the future means being responsible not just for your own health but the well-being of the world you live in. We've gotta eat more local produce and stop relying on industrial farming and animal agriculture. No more strawberries in winter. No more mystery chicken made from pink paste. No more meat in every single meal. Given what we know about the low-quality standards, terrible work conditions, and negative impact on the environment, the current meat industry is beyond repair. Consumer demand needs to shift in the direction of seasonal fruits and vegetables, not just for our own health but for the health of the planet. Flying cherries in from Chile makes about as much fucking sense as raising animals in cages they can't even turn around in. It's time to stop supporting industries that cause such harm. We have to face uncomfortable truths today so we can have a healthier and happier tomorrow.

HOW TO USE THIS BOOK

So sure, this book is full of some first-rate recipes and killer photography, but our books always are. This time around we also wanted to show you how to stock your pantry and store produce to make it last longer. If we call for an ingredient you're not familiar with or the store is sold out, we give you substitutions. We didn't just give you shortcuts, we're giving you the whole fucking road map from pantry to prep to pairings to plating. We've given you the recipes, but what we really want to teach you is how to cook with what you already have on hand. To know what to substitute and how to do it so that meals that begin as recipes start to feel instinctive and always turn out tasting great.

This time we've added a produce glossary in the back that breaks down a lot of shit you probably never knew (but most def should) about all the fresh stuff in your local market. That way, when those seasonal sales hit you can buy artichokes, or whatever you want, with confidence that you've read up on 'em long before they ended up in your cart.

Even the most basic fruits and veggies you're familiar with are low-key superfoods that don't get enough love.

You don't need to waste a whole paycheck on acai when you know just how amazing bell peppers and cilantro are with a lil finesse. You don't need ancient grains or far-out fruits to be healthy. The entire produce section is full of incredible things that you just haven't learned about yet. This book will arm you with all the info you need so you'll never experience produce panic again. And the more you know, the less

ICON GUIDE

freezer friendly

good for leftovers

weeknight go-tos, one-pot meals

gluten-free

pantry staples

longer cooking times, dinner party favs

likely you are to let everything in your fridge rot. Not when you know the kind of magic you've got sittin in there.

Now is the time to be bold. Now is the time to try new shit and stop worrying if this means you have to be anything other than yourself.

IT'S TIME TO EAT LIKE YOU GIVE A FUCK.

Taking your health and what you eat seriously doesn't mean you have to suddenly become a stuck-up asshole who's no fun to be around. Keep your dumbass sense of humor but just eat less trash. These things aren't in opposition, and don't let some self-righteous shithead tell you any different. Being in charge of what you eat means you're in charge of who you're becoming. You are shaping your future. The food you eat quite literally becomes your body so you're gonna want some building blocks that won't crumble with a little breeze. Real food and no filler. Every journey starts with a small step, so come on in and cook with us. Wash your hands. There are aprons behind the door if you need one. Grab a sharp knife and a dish rag. And if you ain't cooking, you're cleanin'.

WELCOME TO A BRAVE NEW MEAL.

BREAKING BED

BREAKFAST

20 - 101: How to Milk

23 - Apple Mormon Muffins

24 - Breakfast Spaghetti

27 - Blueberry-Thyme Marble Rolls

29 - 101: How to Knead

30 - Artichoke Brunch Bake

32 - Orange Cinnamon Morning Rolls

35 - Buckwheat Persimmon Pancakes

36 - Blackberry Sage Oat Bars

37 - Whatever Grain Porridge

38 - Pumpkin Scones

39 - Cowboy Scramble

40 - Maple Kumquat Preserves

43 - Brussels Sprout Hash

HOW TO MILK

Here we've got two options for you: the best milk and the lazy milk. Either way, these are way better than store-bought, and it's way easier to stock up on nuts and nut butters than it is to store a ton of almond milk. Stop going to the store all the damn time and milk your own nuts.

COOK TIME
15 MIN

» **Makes about 6 cups**

2 cups nuts like almond, cashew, macadamia, or a mix

5 cups water

¼ teaspoon salt

1 teaspoon vanilla extract*

1 tablespoon pure maple syrup or your favorite liquid sweetener*

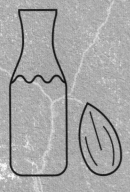

THE BEST NUT MILK

1 Rinse the nuts and stick them in a large jar. Cover with at least 4 inches of water. They're gonna expand as they soak, so make sure your jar has enough room. Let them soak overnight or for at least 8 hours. Short on time? You can soak them in hot water for 2 hours, but the milk won't be as creamy.

2 When the nuts are good and soaked, drain and rinse them. Throw them into your blender with the 5 cups water, salt, and vanilla and maple syrup if you're using them. You'll probably hafta do this shit in batches unless you have a massive blender, and if you do then la dee fuckin dah for you. Let the blender run for at least 1½ minutes because you really want all the nuts broken up and creamy.

3 Use a clean, old cotton shirt, dish towel, or expensive nut milk bag to strain this into whatever you're gonna store it in. If you're big blender gang, you def have those pricey nut milk bags laying around. Just pour the milk over whatever you're using to strain it, carefully gather the corners, and twist until you've got this weird nut milk udder. Now squeeze that shit until it feels like you got all the liquid out and you just have a shirt filled with nut pulp. Sexy.

4 Store the liquid in the fridge and it should keep for a week. It might separate while it sits, but that's natural. A good shake will have it looking good as new.

* Optional but delicious.

Sometimes you wake up and realize you have fuck all to put in your coffee. There's no time for soaking and barely time for blending. This is your SOS milk. It's tasty and works in a pinch but nothing compares to the longer version.

THE EASIER BUT NOT AS DELICIOUS NUT MILK

Throw the nut butter, water, vanilla, and maple syrup into the blender and run it for at least a minute to get all creamy. Store this in the fridge and it will keep for a week.

* Optional but barely.

COOK TIME
5 MIN

》 **Makes 2 cups**

¼ cup almond or cashew butter

2 cups water

½ teaspoon vanilla extract*

1 teaspoon pure maple syrup or your favorite liquid sweetener*

RISE AND SHINE WITH A
FUCKLOAD OF FIBER

This recipe is based on the famous muffins from Rainbow Acres grocery store outside Ogden, Utah, which are legendary in the West. You've never had a muffin until you've hammered down one of these perfectly moist motherfuckers. And now without all the dairy and eggs, you, too, can eat enough fiber in one sitting to kill a horse.

APPLE MORMON MUFFINS

1 In a small bowl, mix the baking soda with the boiling water and set it aside. In a cup, mix the vinegar into the milk and set that shit aside, too.

2 In a bowl, with an electric mixer (or just a whisk and some goddamn willpower), whip the butter until it starts to look fluffy, 3 to 5 minutes. Add the sugar and ground flaxseeds and beat until incorporated. Okay, we're done with the beating.

3 Stir in the milk mixture, flour, salt, and cinnamon and mix again until everything is combined. Add the baking soda/water very slowly and don't fucking burn yourself. Make sure that's all incorporated again. Gently fold in the bran flakes, wheat germ, walnuts, and apples. You can bake these bran-filled fuckers now or you can let the batter sit overnight in the fridge for an even better muffin. Up to you.

4 Warm up your oven to 350°F. Grease up or line your deepest-cup muffin tin.

5 Fill up each cup as high as you can, then stick these dense motherfuckers in the oven until they're golden on top and a toothpick stuck in one comes out clean, 30 to 40 minutes. Let them cool for at least 15 minutes before eating. These are best eaten within the first 4 days, but if you store them in the fridge they'll last at least 1 week.

COOK TIME
60 MIN

» **Makes 12 big or 18 regular-sized muffins**

1 tablespoon baking soda

1 cup boiling water

2 teaspoons apple cider vinegar or lemon juice

1¾ cups almond or other nondairy milk

¼ cup nondairy butter or coconut oil, at room temperature

1 cup cane sugar

2 tablespoons ground flaxseeds

2½ cups all-purpose flour

½ teaspoon salt

1 teaspoon ground cinnamon

2 cups bran flakes

1 cups wheat germ

½ cup walnuts or pecans, chopped

2 apples, chopped (about 2 cups)

>> **Makes enough for 4 to 6 people**

16 ounces uncooked spaghetti

1 tablespoon olive oil

1 yellow onion, sliced into 2-inch-long pieces

2 cups diced tomatoes, fresh or canned with the juices drained away

2 cups grated zucchini or chopped spinach

4 garlic cloves, minced

½ teaspoon salt

1 pound firm tofu

1 tablespoon soy sauce, tamari, or Bragg Liquid Aminos*

1 tablespoon smoked paprika

1 tablespoon all-purpose seasoning

2 teaspoons dried oregano

¾ cup nutritional yeast (nooch)**

2 tablespoons lemon juice

½ cup chopped fresh herbs, like parsley or basil, optional

WTF? See page 180.

**WTF? See page 181.*

It's unfair and unclear why spaghetti has been left out of breakfast. Unfortunately, our search for the truth was stonewalled by local authorities telling us to "please stop calling" and "there's no such thing as a breakfast food press conference." Clearly the government doesn't want you to have spaghetti for breakfast. So guess what the fuck you're gonna do?

BREAKFAST SPAGHETTI

1 Cook the spaghetti according to the package because they know their shit. Before you drain it, scoop out ½ cup of the salted pasta water and set it aside.

2 In a large skillet, warm the oil over medium heat. Add the onion and cook until it starts to look golden around the edges, about 5 minutes. Add the tomatoes and zucchini and cook for 3 to 4 minutes, until everything is starting to soften. Add the garlic and salt and sauté for about 30 seconds.

3 While that shit is going on, drain the tofu and squeeze out as much water as possible. You can squeeze it with your hands; no need to press this fucker. Crumble that tofu into the pan in chunks no bigger than the size of a quarter. Some small bits are best, but the more you stir it the more the tofu chunks are gonna break down so it'll all work out. Sauté that tofu around and try to get it all mixed in for about 3 minutes. If the pan starts looking dry, add a splash of water and move the fuck on with breakfast.

4 Sprinkle in the soy sauce, then add the smoked paprika, seasoning, and oregano and mix all that shit up so everything is coated. Fold in the pasta, the pasta water, nooch, and lemon juice. Let the mixture cook together for about 2 minutes so all the flavors blend and a sauce starts to form. Turn off the heat and sprinkle in the fresh herbs if you're doing all that. Then breakfast is served, bitches.

IT'S NEVER TOO EARLY
TO GET TWISTED

Look at that fucking photo. Why are you still reading this? The ingredients and shit are below. You could have those rolls in your life right now. LOOK AT THAT SHIT. Why the fuck are you still reading? If you're still reading this instead of cooking, maybe you don't deserve them.

» Makes 12 rolls

BLUEBERRY-THYME MARBLE ROLLS

1 In a stand mixer fitted with the paddle (or a big bowl if you're doing this shit by hand), mix together the warm milk, yeast, and sugar and let it sit for a couple of minutes to make sure your yeast is still alive. It will start looking less like individual granules and will start to swell up a little, float, and look kinda like pond scum. If your milk was too hot or the yeast is old as hell, this won't happen and you should just start over with new yeast and milk. There's no fixing that.

2 Once we know all your shit is alive and well, add 4 tablespoons of the butter, the salt, and 1 cup of the flour. Beat on low speed for 30 seconds to get that flour worked in. Scrape down the sides of the bowl with a spatula, then add the remaining 2 cups flour. Beat on medium speed until a smooth dough comes together and pulls away from the sides of the bowl, about 2 minutes. If you're doing this by hand, use a large spoon or rubber spatula. It's not hard, just a bit of an arm workout.

3 Once a ball of dough has come together, you need to knead that fucker. Either keep the dough in the mixer and beat with a dough hook on medium-high for an additional 5 minutes or knead by hand on a lightly floured surface for 5 to 8 minutes. Don't know how to knead? We got you, see page 29.

4 Once you've got a smooth ball of dough going, lightly grease a large bowl with some oil and put the dough ball in there, rubbing it around so it's coated in a little oil, too. Cover the

1 cup almond or oat milk, warm but not hot

1 envelope dry yeast (2¼ teaspoons)

2 tablespoons sugar

6 tablespoons nondairy butter, at room temperature, or olive oil

1 teaspoon salt

3 cups all-purpose flour or bread flour

⅓ cup Blueberry-Thyme Preserves (page 190) or your favorite jam

1 teaspoon chopped fresh thyme—optional, but it's in the title for a fucking reason

(continued)

bowl with a small kitchen towel or some plastic wrap and stick it in a warmish, nonbreezy place to rise. It's gonna get super big, puffy, and double in size, so make sure you picked the right bowl. Depending on how warm your spot is this could take anywhere from 45 minutes to 1½ hours.

5 Grease a 9 × 13-inch baking pan or two 9-inch square or round baking pans and line the bottoms with parchment. Punch the dough down to release the air and place it on a well-floured surface. Roll it out until you have a 10 × 15-inch rectangle, a little bigger than a piece of paper. Cut that rectangle in half crosswise and spread a thin layer of jam all over one half. Now cover that shit up with the other half of the dough, leaving you with a 5 × 15-inch rectangle of dough with a preserve filling. Now cut that dough lengthwise into 4 strips and cut each of those strips crosswise into thirds, leaving you with 12 strips of dough 5 inches long and about 1¼ inches wide.

6 To get the marble shape, grab a preserve-filled strip and hold each end in a different hand. Twist the dough twice and then make a U with the strip. Fold the left strip over the right and then stuff the end of the right strip over the left and through the center of the small circle you just made. Tuck the other end underneath and you should get something looking like a little marbled knot. It's just like a short, single knot on a shoelace with the ends tucked in and under. Don't overthink this part. Place these in the baking pan(s) with at least 1 inch between them because these fuckers expand. Once you're done, cover the pan(s), and let rise again until they're all puffy and looking like rolls, another 30 to 45 minutes.

7 Warm up your oven to 350°F.

8 Melt the remaining 2 tablespoons butter. Brush the rolls with some of the melted butter and sprinkle with the thyme. Bake until golden brown on top, 20 to 25 minutes, rotating the pan(s) front to back halfway through. When they are ready, pull them out and brush them with a little more butter. Let them cool for a few minutes before serving. To store, cover the rolls and store at room temperature for 2 to 3 days or in the refrigerator for up to 1 week.

HOW TO KNEAD

There are plenty of videos out there that show you how to do this, but we are here for you if the power is out.

Sprinkle some flour on a big, clean nontextured surface like your countertop (if that shit isn't tile), your kitchen table, or a cutting board. The flour will keep your dough from sticking so even though it's kinda a big fucking mess, just do it. Plop the dough out onto the floured surface and sprinkle some more flour on top of it.

Now it's down to the real shit. Push the dough down and out and away from you using the heels of your hands. Kinda like those old-timey cartoons when you see them using a washboard, if that makes any fucking sense. This is stretching out the gluten strands of your dough so when that fucker rises in the oven it can stand up instead of just collapsing back in on itself, so yeah, it's important.

Fold the dough in half, kinda turning it a quarter-turn clockwise toward you as you do it. Then press out again, and keep going for about 3 minutes. Yeah, that's a long fucking time, but a lot of recipes call for 10 to 15 minutes, so you're fucking welcome. Sprinkle it with a little more flour if it starts sticking to your surface as you knead.

Continue kneading until the dough comes together in a sort of smooth-looking ball, 4 to 5 minutes total. Coat it in olive oil so it doesn't dry out while it rises and then let it do its thing all covered up while you clean up the flour you got all over your fucking kitchen. Check your ass, because you always end up with a weird flour handprint on there, trust us.

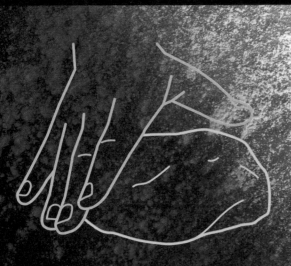

COOK TIME 80 MIN

》Makes enough for 2 as a main, 4 as a side

2 cups chickpea flour*

½ teaspoon garlic powder

½ teaspoon kosher salt

3 cups water

¼ cup extra virgin olive oil

1 shallot, minced

1 cup sliced canned or jarred artichoke hearts

1 tablespoon chopped fresh dill, plus more for serving

Black pepper

Some of y'all are looking at this recipe and thinking, "A bake for brunch?" YEAH BITCH, WHAT ABOUT IT? You already know what a frittata is. This is that, just without all the egg.

ARTICHOKE BRUNCH BAKE

1 In a medium bowl, combine the chickpea flour, garlic powder, and salt. Gradually add the water, whisking constantly, until a smooth, thin batter forms. Leave that shit alone for at least 1 hour while you make some coffee and fix your face so people think you just wake up beautiful.

2 While the batter mixture is sitting, position an oven rack in the second highest slot and crank your oven to 500°F.

3 Pour the oil into a large cast-iron skillet or other heavy ovensafe pan and swirl it around so it coats the bottom. Add the shallot and artichoke hearts and swirl around one more time. Grab that batter you've had sitting around and skim off any foam or similar bullshit that's floating on top. Then stir the fresh dill into the batter and pour it into the skillet. Stir gently to evenly mix and so you get some oil on top of the batter. Crack some fresh black pepper over the top if you wanna be fancy (which clearly you do 'cause you're cooking this shit).

4 Throw the skillet in the oven and bake until it no longer jiggles in the center and looks browned around the edges, 10 to 12 minutes. If your broiler is on top of your oven, turn that to high for the last 2 minutes to get the cake all golden on top.

5 Let it cool for a couple minutes to fully set, then serve warm or at room temperature with some more fresh dill on top.

It's just dried, powdered chickpeas. It's fucking delicious and a good way to get extra protein into your dishes. Can't find it? Check near the tahini or in the spice aisle. Still no luck? The Internet exists.

》 **Makes 8 rolls, enough for 1 to 8 people**

1½ cups plus 1 tablespoon almond milk

1 envelope dry yeast (2¼ teaspoons)

½ cup cane sugar

4 cups all-purpose flour

1½ teaspoons ground cinnamon

½ teaspoon ground cardamom*

½ teaspoon salt

2 tablespoons ground golden flaxseeds**

5 tablespoons nondairy butter, melted

Grated zest of 1 orange (about 1 tablespoon)

3 tablespoons pure maple syrup

Sesame seeds, for garnish

Yeah, these take some time, but there's nothing better in the morning than fresh rolls. The orange and cinnamon in here are so fucking good but subtle enough that people won't be able to tell exactly why they can't stop eating them. Trust us, we've eaten our weight in rolls.

ORANGE CINNAMON MORNING ROLLS

1 In a small pan, heat 1 cup of the almond milk to just warm but not scalding. Think coffee you left out on the counter for a little while—warmish but not hot at all. Pour this into a bowl and stir the yeast into it with a pinch of the sugar and set it aside. Once you see it looking a little foamy at the top of the glass, it means your yeast is alive and you're good to go. Not foamy? It's dead and so are your chances at making this recipe unless your ass gets new yeast.

2 In a stand mixer with the dough hook, stir together the remaining sugar, the flour, cinnamon, cardamom, and salt until they're all mixed up. (You could do this all by hand if you don't have a stand mixer, so don't quit. You're just gonna need to put in some work when it comes to kneading, but that will offset the carbs, we swear.)

3 In a small glass, whisk together the remaining ½ cup almond milk and ground flaxseeds until a watery paste forms. Set it aside.

4 Make a well in the center of the flour mixture and pour in the yeast mixture, flax mixture, 4 tablespoons of the melted butter, and the orange zest. Beat the mixture on low, scraping down the sides as needed, until a dough forms. Beat on high until the dough looks smooth and has a little stretch to it when you try to tear a small piece apart, 5 to 7 minutes. If the dough is too sticky and isn't forming a ball, add a little more flour while it's being kneaded, a couple of tablespoons at a time until it shapes up. Too dry-lookin'? Do the same shit but with almond milk. (Doing this by hand? Beat all the ingredients in with a large spoon, then turn the dough out onto a well-floured surface and knead for about 15 minutes. Don't know how the fuck to knead? We anticipated this; see page 33.)

5 When the dough is looking good, place it in an oiled bowl, turning once to coat the top so it doesn't dry out. Cover with a kitchen towel or some plastic wrap and let it rise in a warm place until it roughly doubles in size, 1 to 1½ hours. You'll know.

6 Grab a 9 × 13-inch baking pan and grease and flour it. When the dough is looking good, punch it down, yeah exactly how it sounds, and divide the dough into 8 roughly even pieces. Roll them into tight balls and place them, seam side down, in the baking pan. Now let this rise one more time in a warm place, with a clean kitchen towel over them, until the rolls have expanded and are all kinda touchin' and fluffy looking, about 30 minutes. Meanwhile, preheat the oven to 375°F.

7 While the rolls are rising for the second time, in a small bowl, mix together the maple syrup and the remaining 1 tablespoon melted butter and remaining 1 tablespoon milk.

8 When ready to put the rolls in the oven, brush that maple shit over the top of all the rolls and sprinkle with sesame seeds if you want to look extra fancy. Place this in the oven and bake until the tops of the rolls are golden brown, 15 to 20 minutes. Let them cool for at least 15 minutes before serving.

Don't wanna buy it? Leave it out or replace with more cinnamon.

*** You can use regular ground brown flaxseeds here, but the golden ones just look nicer and less health food–ish because there isn't a ton of brown shit in your rolls. If you're feeding these fuckers to kids, that shit matters.*

Wanna do some of this shit ahead of time? Make the dough the night before, shape them in the baking pan, cover it, and stick that fucker in the fridge to rise its last time overnight. When you warm up the oven in the morning to get baking, pull them out, let them warm up for 10 minutes on the counter, then brush them with the maple stuff, like nothing happened. You can also bake a big batch and freeze a ton of them for later.

HAS FOOD EVER
AWOKEN SOMETHING
SEXUAL IN YOU?

Let's take some basic shit everyone knows already, pancakes, and introduce a couple ingredients you never use. Sounds helluva lot fancier this way. Invite some friends over for brunch and charge them. They'll pay . . . these are THAT GOOD.

BUCKWHEAT PERSIMMON PANCAKES

1 In a medium bowl, add the ground flaxseed, milk, and vinegar, stir, then leave that shit alone while you get everything else ready. In another medium bowl, stir together the flour, baking powder, baking soda, cinnamon, ginger, and salt.

2 In the bowl with the milk mixture, add the mashed persimmon and whisk that fucker up until everything is combined. Slowly pour the wet ingredients into the dry ingredients and stir until it's mostly all mixed up and there aren't any big dry clumps. Batter done.

3 Now if you don't know how to cook a fucking pancake, we got you, but for real, examine your life. Warm up a greased griddle or big skillet over medium heat. Add about ¼ cup of batter and cook for 3 to 5 minutes on each side, until lightly browned. On the first side you'll know it's time to flip when the bubbles start showing through the pancake in the center and the edge retains its shape. Repeat until all of the batter is used up, then serve warm with more cut-up persimmons and maple syrup.

COOK TIME 20 MIN

》Makes about 8 to 10

2 tablespoon ground flaxseed

1¾ cups unsweetened nondairy milk

1 teaspoon apple cider vinegar or lemon juice

1½ cup buckwheat flour or all-purpose flour

2 teaspoons baking powder

1 teaspoon baking soda

1 teaspoon ground cinnamon

½ teaspoon ground ginger

¼ teaspoon salt

3 medium persimmons, mashed (about ¾ cup), plus 1 persimmon, diced, for serving

1 tablespoon coconut oil or nondairy butter

Pure maple syrup, for serving

》 **Makes about 9, depending on how you cut them**

BLACKBERRY FILLING

2 cups chopped blackberries*

1 tablespoon minced fresh sage**

1 tablespoon fresh lemon juice

1 tablespoon cane sugar

1 teaspoon vanilla extract

OAT BASE

3 cups rolled oats

⅓ cup almond butter or peanut butter if that's all you got

⅓ cup refined coconut oil

¼ cup brown sugar

1½ teaspoons baking soda

1½ teaspoons vanilla extract

¼ teaspoon salt

1 teaspoon cornstarch

Handful of sliced almonds (optional)

* Cherries or raspberries would be great in here, too. Just leave out the sage in that case.

** This is optional, but live a little.

Still eating those dry crumb-bomb breakfast bars? Make your own and see how fucking simple that shit is to throw together. The only thing that should be crumbling is your rapidly fleeting youth, not your breakfast.

BLACKBERRY SAGE OAT BARS

1 Warm up your oven to 350°F. Grease an 8 × 8-inch baking dish and line it with parchment paper.

2 First, make the filling: In a small bowl, mix together the blackberries, sage, lemon juice, sugar, and vanilla and let it sit while you make the oat base.

3 Make the oat base: In a food processor, combine the oats, almond butter, coconut oil, brown sugar, baking soda, vanilla, and salt. Pulse that shit for a few seconds until there aren't any whole oats but that shit is still coarser than flour. Scoop out two-thirds of that mixture and press it in an even layer into your prepared pan, you know, like you're making fucking bars. It's not that hard.

4 Pour off the juice that has been released by the blackberries, then toss them with the cornstarch. Spread them gently and evenly on top of the oat base. Crumble the last one-third of the oat mixture over the blackberries and gently press into an even layer. Sprinkle the almonds on top (if using) and throw that shit in the oven.

5 Bake until the top and edges start looking kinda golden, 35 to 45 minutes. Let cool completely in the pan before taking out and cutting into bars. Store the bars in the fridge to help them keep their shape if it's a hot-ass summer.

You thought porridge was just for fairy-tale characters? Shit, use your imagination, serve this in a misshaped bowl with an eccentric spoon. Why not start your day creating your own magical nonsense? It definitely beats what fresh hell reality is gonna serve you today.

WHATEVER GRAIN PORRIDGE

1 In a large stockpot, heat the oil over medium heat. Add the rice, quinoa, oats, millet, and salt. Stir all that around and cook until the grains smell kinda toasty, about 2 minutes. Add the water and bring that whole mess to a boil. Once it's boiling, reduce the heat to medium-low, partially cover, and let the pot simmer. Stir the pot every now and then and let it cook until the grains are soft and the pot starts getting thick like oatmeal, 30 to 45 minutes. Turn off the heat and stir in the milk.

2 Serve hot with some brown sugar or maple syrup on top and whatever fresh fruit is hanging around. No fresh fruit? Swirl in some of our Blueberry-Thyme Preserves (page 190) or Maple Kumquat Preserves (page 40) and toss in some toasted nuts. No matter what you do, you'll be full and happy all motherfucking morning.

COOK TIME
45 MIN

>> **Makes enough for 4 people**

1 tablespoon olive oil

½ cup brown rice

½ cup quinoa

½ cup steel-cut oats

¼ cup millet

½ teaspoon salt

5 cups water

1 cup almond or your favorite nondairy milk

» **Makes 8 big-ass scones**

3¼ cups whole wheat pastry flour or all-purpose flour

½ cup brown sugar, plus more for sprinkling

1 tablespoon baking powder

½ teaspoon salt

½ teaspoon ground cinnamon

½ teaspoon ground ginger

¼ teaspoon ground nutmeg

1 can full-fat coconut milk, about 1½ cups

1 cup pureed pumpkin or butternut squash*

2 tablespoons pure maple syrup

1 tablespoon vanilla extract

½ cup chopped walnuts or almonds (optional)

For brushing: Grapeseed oil, olive oil, pure maple syrup, or almond milk

Ya feel that? The air is kinda crisp this morning. It's still warm out but you see brave co-workers tryin' to pull off a scarf. Love it or hate it, pumpkin-spice season approaches. Lattes are fine but it's really just pricey anxiety. Which is why we suggest scones. Not only do you get to flex on the fall trend, but you also feel full. Start the holiday season right and get sconed.

PUMPKIN SCONES

1 Warm up the oven to 425°F. Line a baking sheet with some parchment paper.

2 In a large bowl, whisk together the flour, brown sugar, baking powder, salt, and spices. In a medium bowl, combine the coconut milk, pumpkin, maple syrup, and vanilla and whisk that shit together until it is smooth. Having trouble? Blend that bitch with an immersion blender.

3 Make a hole in the center of the dry ingredients and pour in the pumpkin/milk mixture. Stir until all the flour is mostly mixed and then fold in the nuts (if using). Shape the dough into a ball in the bowl using your hands and then move it to your baking sheet.

4 Pat down the dough into a round no more than 1½ inches high. Take a sharp knife and cut that fucker up into 8 wedges (like a pizza). Don't move them apart or anything. They'll all stick back together, but this will make it look cool and it'll be way easier to cut later. Brush the outside with a little oil, maple syrup, or milk. Sprinkle a little extra sugar for looks.

5 Stick that shit in the oven until a toothpick stuck in the center comes out clean, 20 to 30 minutes.

* Just skin, chop up, and steam a little pumpkin or butternut squash until tender and toss in the blender or mash it up real good until you get 1 cup. Easy peasy, motherfucker. Or yeah, just use a can.

This recipe is so slick it comes with its own Marty Robbins ballad. This recipe just flipped over a poker table and shot the hat clean off a man's head. This fucking recipe just rolled a cigarette one-handed. Get your day going with some goddamn grit.

COWBOY SCRAMBLE

1 Chop up the potatoes, skin on, into pieces no larger than a nickel. Chop the onion and bell pepper into pea-sized pieces. Shred the carrot on a box grater and mince the garlic.

2 Warm the oil in a large skillet over medium heat. Add the potatoes and onion with a pinch of salt and cook until the onions look a little golden and potatoes soften up a little, 8 to 10 minutes. If the pan starts looking dry, add a tablespoon or two of water to get that shit moving again. Now add the bell pepper and cook for 3 to 4 minutes until it's all looking tender. Now add the garlic and sauté for 30 seconds.

3 While that shit is going on, drain the tofu and squeeze out as much water as possible with your hands. Now crumble that tofu into the pan in chunks about the size of a quarter. Some small bits are cool, so don't stress if it's not all uniform. Sauté that tofu around and try to get it all mixed in for about 5 minutes. If the pan starts looking dry again, add a splash of water and move the fuck on with breakfast. Add the soy sauce and lemon juice all over the pan and stir. Add the grated carrot, dried basil, cumin, paprika, nooch, and hot sauce right after and stir those fuckers in. Let this all cook together for about 2 minutes so that all the flavors blend. Pour in the cheese sauce, stir until it's all mixed in, then turn off the heat. Taste and see if it needs more hot sauce, salt, or spice. That's on you.

4 Serve warm topped with green onions, cilantro, jalapeños, and chunks of avocado. Extra hot sauce on the side, obvs.

COOK TIME 25 MIN

》 **Enough for 4 to 6 people**

5 red new potatoes

1 white onion

1 red bell pepper

1 carrot

4 garlic cloves

1 tablespoon olive oil

Salt

1 pound of extra-firm tofu

1 tablespoon soy sauce, tamari, or Bragg Liquid Aminos*

2 tablespoons lemon or lime juice

2 teaspoons dried basil

1 teaspoon ground cumin

1 teaspoon paprika

¼ cup nutritional yeast (nooch)**

3 teaspoons of your favorite hot sauce

1 cup cashew cheese sauce (page 213)

Garnish: sliced green onions, chopped cilantro, sliced jalapeños, avocado

* WTF? See page 180.

** WTF? See page 181.

>> **Makes about 2 cups**

1 pound kumquats, sliced*

½ cup cane sugar

1 cup pure maple syrup

½ vanilla bean,** split open lengthwise

If your kumquats are small, slice them in half lengthwise and flick out any big seeds. If your kumquats are thicker than your thumb, cut them into slices crosswise, also flicking out any big seeds. It's totally okay to have a mix of cuts in the same pot. This shit is very forgiving. You should end up with roughly 4 cups of cut-up kumquats.

Kumquats are like tiny little oranges and you can eat those cute fuckers whole. They are weird and delicious and worth buying if you ever find them in your store. These preserves are great on our Orange Cinnamon Morning Rolls (page 32), any kind of vanilla cake, swirled into oatmeal, and spread over buttered sourdough toast with some chopped pistachios on top. Basically, they go on anything.

MAPLE KUMQUAT PRESERVES

1 Place the kumquats and sugar in a deep saucepan over medium heat. Let this cook for a minute or two until the sugar starts to dissolve around the kumquats, then stir in the maple syrup. If you're using a vanilla bean, scrape the vanilla seeds into the pan and add the vanilla pod, too. Bring this sweet smelling cauldron to a boil, then reduce the heat to low. Let this simmer, stirring often, until the kumquats all look kinda translucent and the liquid in the pot is thick and syrupy, 25 to 30 minutes. The only way you can mess this up is by forgetting to stir this shit and letting it burn or boil over. Otherwise, we know you nailed it.

2 Remove from the heat and let this motherfucker cool completely before putting it in a glass jar with a lid and sticking this in the fridge. It should last in there for at least 1 month.

** Optional but classy-as-fuck touch. You can add 1 teaspoon vanilla extract if that's what you've got.

EVOLVE PAST AVOCADO TOAST

SPROUT A NEW BRUNCH FAV

So we don't hafta repeat ourselves, check out the Brussels sprout section of this book (page 224). Did you see the part where we talk about how overcooking these little bastards can change the taste? Glad you're paying attention. Now that you're educated on how to properly prepare 'em, enter this goddamn delectable hash into your brunch rotation. What's that? You don't have a brunch rotation? That was the old you who hated Brussels sprouts.

BRUSSELS SPROUT HASH

In a large skillet, warm up the oil over medium-high heat. Add the onion and cook until it starts looking golden brown, 6 to 8 minutes. Drizzle in the Bragg's and stir the pot around so that all the onions get a little. Add the Brussels sprouts and a pinch of salt and occasionally stir until browned and tender, another 5 to 8 minutes. If the pan starts looking a little dry, add a tablespoon or two of water. When the sprouts are looking right, drizzle the lemon juice on top and season with salt and pepper. Top with the panko and serve right away.

* WTF? See page 180.

COOK TIME 25 MIN

>> **Makes enough for 4 as a side**

2 tablespoons olive oil

1 large yellow onion, chopped

1 tablespoon Bragg Liquid Aminos*

1 pound Brussels sprouts, shredded or thinly sliced

Salt

Juice of ½ lemon or 1 tablespoon Fresh Chile Vinegar (page 211)

Black pepper

½ cup Panko Pasta Topping (page 205; optional but always worth it)

CRAVEABLE CORNERSTONES

SOUPS & SALADS

101: HOW TO PREPARE NUTS	46
SHAVED ASPARAGUS AND CHIVE SALAD	47
SMOKE CABBAGE AND TOMATO STEW WITH TORTELLINI	48
ARUGULA AND FENNEL SALAD SALAD WITH PRESERVED LEMON VINAIGRETTE	50
SOUTHWESTERN SLAW	51
SMASHED CUCUMBER SALAD	53
SHREDDED DAIKON SALAD	54
CARROT AND RICE SOUP	55
ROMAINE HEARTS SALAD WITH HORSERADISH AND DILL DRESSING AND HOMEMADE OLD BAY CROUTONS	56
FRIED CAPERS	58
CREAMY CURRIED PARSNIP SOUP	59
TOMATILLO AND CUCUMBER GAZPACHO	61
SWEET POTATO COCONUT SOUP WITH GINGER	62

HOW TO PREPARE NUTS

We use a lot of nuts in this book, so we thought we'd give you a heads-up on how to handle them. First, raw nuts have lots of oil in them, which means if you just store them wherever the fuck you want, like your hot-ass pantry, they'll spoil. Throw these expensive motherfuckers in your freezer so they'll last longer and you can get your money's worth.

TOASTING NUTS AND SEEDS

Second, throughout the book we ask you to use toasted nuts, so we thought we should walk you through that shit. And yes, all these tips go for seeds like shelled sunflower seeds too. Buying pretoasted nuts is such a fucking waste of money, so do like we do and get toasted at home. There are two ways to do this: The stovetop method, which is easier and faster, or the oven method, which is better for large batches. Whichever one you choose: DON'T. EVER. FUCKING. WANDER. AWAY. while you're toasting nuts. These oily little bastards burn in a hot second, so don't toast your money because you got distracted. Also, toast the nuts before you chop them up. The smaller the nuts, the faster they toast and the easier they are to burn. Stay put until they're done and you'll be getting down on deez nuts in no time. GOT 'EM.

METHOD 1: STOVETOP

Heat a large skillet or sauté pan over medium-high heat. Add the nuts in a single layer and then stir those sons of bitches frequently until the nuts turn golden brown and start smelling, well, nutty. Remove from the heat and pour those fuckers onto a plate to cool. If you leave them in the hot pan, even with the stove off, they'll probably burn. We're speaking from personal experience, so learn from our fuck-ups.

METHOD 2: OVEN

Preheat the oven to 350°F and pull out a sheet pan. Spread the nuts out in an even layer and stick that shit in the oven. Roast them for 5 minutes, then pull them out, stir them around, and stick them back in for another 2 or 3 minutes to even out that roast. Depending on the nuts you're using, you might need to roast them for another 5 to 8 minutes, but until you get good at this shit you'll wanna check every couple minutes so those bitches don't burn. They're done when they look all golden and smell all extra nut-like. Pull them out and pour them on a plate to stop the cooking. Fucking done.

Anyone can assemble a salad, it's not that fucking hard. But serving a shaved asparagus salad? Now that shit looks impressive. You could use more asparagus in your diet anyway. Asparagus has a ton of fiber, vitamins, folate, and this shit called glutathione, which breaks down harmful compounds like free radicals and carcinogens, making asparagus a powerful weapon to protect yourself from lung, bone, breast, and colon cancer. So, this salad is really just a tasty shield.

SHAVED ASPARAGUS AND CHIVE SALAD

1 Grab a large bowl and mix together the oil, lemon juice, and garlic in the bottom and set it aside.

2 Grab your asparagus and chop the bottom inch off all the spears. That shit is just too tough and ya look like a goddamn rabbit trying to chew a veggie for that long. Grab a single spear, hold it down on a cutting board and, using your vegetable peeler, peel a long strip of it off like you're peeling a carrot. Do each side a couple of times until you are left with a kinda thin strip. Do this with all the spears. This doesn't need to be perfect, but you're just looking for mostly thin strips.

3 Throw the shaved asparagus into the bowl with the dressing and toss it around a bit. Fold in the greens and chives and toss it around again. Sprinkle in the almonds, salt, and pepper to taste and toss until everything is combined.

4 Serve right away and watch how fucking impressed everyone is.

COOK TIME
10 MIN

» **Makes enough for 2 to 4 people**

2 tablespoons olive oil

2 tablespoons fresh lemon juice

1 clove garlic, minced

1 bunch of asparagus (about 1 pound)

3 cups soft, sweet greens, such as spinach or spring salad mix

2 tablespoons minced fresh chives

⅓ cup chopped toasted almonds (see opposite page)

¼ teaspoon salt

Black pepper

»» **Makes enough for 4 to 6 people**

2 tablespoons olive oil

1 small onion, chopped (about 1½ cups)

2 leeks, sliced (about 2 cups)

2 carrots, chopped (about 1 cup)

3 ribs celery, chopped (about 2 cups)

4 to 5 garlic cloves, minced

1 tablespoon smoked paprika

1 teaspoon dried thyme

1 tablespoon chopped rosemary

2 tablespoons chopped fresh parsley, plus more for garnish

1 can (15 ounces) fire-roasted diced tomatoes

½ head of cabbage, chopped (about 4 cups)

6 cups vegetable broth

¼ cup uncooked black lentils

3 cups fresh tortellini or 2 cups dried small pasta like shells

Juice of ½ lemon

Salt and black pepper

Stew is just a hearty-ass soup and this one is the heartiest. It's chock full of fresh herbs and tons of veggies, so you're getting all the nutrition you need and all the flavor you want.

SMOKY CABBAGE AND TOMATO STEW WITH TORTELLINI

1 Grab a large soup pot and warm it up over medium-high heat. Add the olive oil and once that's all warmed up, throw in the onion. Sauté until the onion starts to get a little golden, 5 to 8 minutes. Add the leeks, carrots, and celery and cook for another 3 minutes so that everything gets warmed up and starts to soften. Now add the garlic, smoked paprika, thyme, rosemary, and parsley. This should smell like the beginnings of soup now, it's that fucking easy. Add the tomatoes, cabbage, broth, and lentils and let it come to a simmer. If you're using pasta instead of tortellini add them when the pot comes to a simmer. Cook until the lentils start to soften, 10 to 15 minutes. If you're using tortellini, add it now and cook until everything is soft and tasty as hell, another 4 to 5 minutes. Remove from the heat, add the lemon juice, and season with salt and pepper until it tastes right to you.

2 Serve right away and top with more fresh parsley for that fancy look.

THE PERFECT THICKNESS
TO CURE YOUR SICKNESS

》Makes enough for 4 people

6 cups arugula, chopped if the leaves are large

2 fist-size bulbs fennel, sliced into thin strips*

¼ cup or more Preserved Lemon Vinaigrette (page 210)

Salt and black pepper

¼ cup chopped toasted almonds**

2 tablespoons chopped fresh parsley or mint (optional)

* Learn more on page 233.

** See How to Toast Nuts, page 46.

This salad is perfect for that weird time between winter and spring when the produce section is looking bare AF. Crunchy from the fennel, peppery from the arugula, and bright from the preserved lemon, this fucker would run $16 at restaurant. Charge your guests $14.

ARUGULA AND FENNEL SALAD WITH PRESERVED LEMON VINAIGRETTE

In a large bowl, toss together the arugula and sliced fennel. Drizzle the vinaigrette on top. Season with salt and pepper and toss until everything looks coated. Fold in the almonds and herbs and serve that shit right away.

Wanna make it extra fancy? Slice an apple or pear into bite-sized pieces and toss it right in.

We love slaw but fucking hate mayo. Enter: avocado. The creaminess of avocado gets slept on because y'all pigeonholed it on toast. Shameful. This southwestern salad has way more flavor than your average deli slaw and way less fat.

SOUTHWESTERN SLAW

1 Make the dressing: Throw all that shit into a blender or food processor and run until it looks smooth. If you have a crappy blender and have trouble getting it going, just add a tablespoon or two of water. Pour into a cup and set aside.

2 Make the slaw: In a large bowl, toss together both cabbages, the bell pepper, carrot, corn kernels, jalapeño, chives, cilantro, and salt. Pour the dressing on top and toss until everything is coated. If you're serving right away, add the pumpkin seeds (if using), otherwise stick that fucker in the fridge and top with the pumpkin seeds right before you put it on the table.

* Either fresh corn scraped off the cob or thawed frozen corn kernels is fine.

COOK TIME
15 MIN

》**Makes enough for 6 as a side**

SOUTHWESTERN DRESSING

1 avocado, sliced

¼ cup chopped green onions (white parts)

½ cup corn kernels*

3 tablespoons fresh lime juice

3 tablespoons rice vinegar

2 tablespoons olive oil

½ teaspoon salt

¼ teaspoon chili powder

¼ cup garlic powder

¼ teaspoon cumin

SLAW

4 cups thinly sliced green cabbage

2 cups thinly sliced red cabbage

1 red bell pepper, thinly sliced

1 carrot, shredded

1 to 1½ cups corn kernels*

1 jalapeño, thinly sliced

½ cup minced fresh chives or green onions

½ cup chopped cilantro

¼ teaspoon salt

1 cup hulled pumpkin seeds (optional), toasted (see page 46)

1 Bird's-Eye Chiles,
see page 228

1 Bird's-Eye Chiles,
see page 228

2 Smashed Cucumber
Salad

3 Shredded Daikon
Salad, page 54

This simple salad is refreshing as fuck anytime but especially when it's hotter than hell outside. This is a perfect side to our Teriyaki Jackfruit with Curry Udon Noodles (page 117).

SMASHED CUCUMBER SALAD

1 Slice the cucumbers in half lengthwise, then chop them up into 1-inch pieces—think smaller than your pinkie finger. Place the cucumbers cut-side down on a cutting board and use the wide side of your knife or a potato masher to kinda gently smash down on the cucumbers. They'll start to crack open, which is exactly what you want. It's all rustic and shit.

2 Place the smashed cucumbers in a bowl and sprinkle them with the salt. Let them sit there for like 15 minutes so that they can release some extra water (that way they take on more of the flavors you're gonna give them in a minute). After a little bit, pour off any water that's seeped out into the bowl. Add the vinegar, sesame oil, soy sauce, garlic, and pepper flakes and stir it all around so that all the cucumbers get coated. Now stick this in the fridge for at least 1 hour so that the cucumbers get enough time to absorb all that flavor. This is perfect to make the night or morning before you're gonna serve it.

COOK TIME
75 MIN

》 **Makes enough for 4 as a side**

4 Persian cucumbers or half an English cucumber

¼ teaspoon salt

1 tablespoon rice vinegar

1 tablespoon toasted sesame oil

1 teaspoon soy sauce

1 clove garlic, minced or grated

¼ teaspoon red pepper flakes or 1 bird's-eye chile, minced (learn more about chiles on pages 226-228)

» **Makes enough for 4 as a side**

2 medium daikon,*
shredded (5 to 6 cups)

1 carrot, shredded
(about 1 cup)

¼ teaspoon salt

⅓ cup green onions,
thinly sliced

1 clove garlic, minced
or finely grated

1-inch piece of
ginger, minced or
finely grated

3 tablespoons rice
vinegar

1 teaspoon tamari or
soy sauce

1 teaspoon toasted
sesame oil

Pinch of cane sugar
(optional, but add
it if you aren't a
radish head)

Sesame seeds,
for garnish

Daikon is the best radish out there and this
salad is a great simple side for when the table
feels a little empty. Pair it with our Sticky Tofu
with Sesame Sauce (page 135) and Pan-Seared Okra
with Lime (page 95) for a bowl that will have your
DMs lighting up when you post the pic.

SHREDDED DAIKON SALAD

Throw the shredded daikon and carrot together in a bowl.
Sprinkle the salt on top and set aside for 5 minutes. Pour out
any water in the bottom of the bowl that might've leached out
from the veggies. Fold in the green onions, garlic, and ginger,
then drizzle with the vinegar, tamari, and sesame oil. Sprinkle a
pinch of cane sugar (if using) on top. Let that chill for at least
30 minutes in the fridge before serving, then top with some
sesame seeds. Maybe you could also chill for half an hour
while you wait. Maybe you sit down in a quiet space and focus
on your breath for a bit. Maybe you meditate, that's like a salad
for your brain.

*Hate daikon or can't find it? Try substituting jicama, which is sweeter and
also goddamn delicious.*

You know carrots have a shitload of health benefits but you don't get them in your diet enough. Oh, you saw some carrot shavings in a salad you ate a month ago? That shit doesn't count. But our carrot and rice soup can help fix that. It's so damn good you'll wanna inject it straight into your bloodstream. DISCLAIMER DO NOT INJECT CARROT SOUP INTO YOUR BLOODSTREAM. Use a spoon, dummy.

CARROT AND RICE SOUP

1 In a large soup pot, heat up the oil over medium heat. Add the onion and sauté until it begins to look golden, 5 to 7 minutes. Add the carrots, celery, garlic, Bragg's, salt, and pepper flakes and stir that around for 1 minute just to get everything all acquainted and shit. Add the rice, stir it up, then pour in the broth. Bring it to a boil, cover, and reduce the heat to a simmer. Let that go until the brown rice is nice and soft, 30 to 40 minutes. If you're using white rice, start checking on it after about 20 minutes 'cause it cooks faster than brown rice.

2 When the rice is tender, stir in the kale, parsley, dill, lemon juice, and black pepper to taste and let it all simmer together until the kale is good and wilted, about 3 more minutes. Taste and add more salt, pepper, or lemon juice if you think it needs it. Serve right away.

* WTF? See page 180.

** If you want to make this a main meal, cut down the rice to ¾ cup and add 1½ cups cooked white beans or chickpeas to the mix. Fiber and protein, baby.

*** Almost any dark, leafy green would work here: spinach, Swiss chard, collards, whateverthefuck you have. Remove any tough stems if you choose a sturdier green.

>> **Makes enough for 4 to 6 people**

1 tablespoon olive oil

1 yellow onion, chopped

3 carrots, chopped

3 ribs celery, chopped

5 garlic cloves, minced

1 teaspoon Bragg Liquid Aminos*

½ teaspoon salt

¼ teaspoon red pepper flakes

1 cup short-grain brown or white rice**

8 cups vegetable broth

3 to 4 cups chopped kale***

⅓ cup chopped fresh parsley

½ cup chopped fresh dill

2 tablespoons fresh lemon juice

Black pepper

**» Makes enough
for 4 to 6 people**

**3 romaine hearts,
chopped into ½-inch
slices, or 1 big head of
romaine or green leaf
lettuce**

2 ribs celery, chopped

**1 Persian cucumber or
½ English cucumber,
sliced**

1 tomato, chopped

½ avocado, chopped

**¼ cup chopped fresh
chives or green onions**

**2 tablespoons minced
fresh dill**

**¼ cup Horseradish
and Dill Dressing
(page 208)**

**¼ recipe Homemade
Old Bay Croutons
(page 187)**

**Quick-Pickled Red
Onions (page 195)**

Salt and black pepper

Once we nailed this recipe down we couldn't get enough. Even the pickiest of people and healthy-eating haters will drool over this dish. Plus it's a solid excuse for you to incorporate more salads into your diet. And obviously, the only stuff you actually need to make this salad is the lettuce, dressing, and croutons. Everything else is fucking awesome but ultimately extra, so use what you've got.

ROMAINE HEARTS SALAD WITH HORSERADISH AND DILL DRESSING AND HOMEMADE OLD BAY CROUTONS

Grab a big-ass bowl and toss together the romaine, celery, cucumber, tomato, avocado, chives, and dill. Drizzle the dressing on top and toss until everything is coated. Fold in the croutons and pickled onions. Season with salt and pepper. Taste and if everything is how you want it, serve it up right away.

1. Homemade Old Bay Croutons, page 187

2. Quick Pickled Red Onions, page 195

3. Tomatoes, see page 247

4. Horseradish and Dill Dressing, page 208

>> **Makes enough
for 2 large salads
or 1 pasta dish**

¼ **cup capers, drained
and patted dry**

2 **tablespoons corn or
rice flour**

2 **tablespoons high-
heat oil, such as
safflower**

All kinds of capers are fucking amazing. Whether
its a heist or pickled flower buds, you need more
capers in your life. Throw these on a salad or
pasta to make things look extra fucking fancy.

FRIED CAPERS

1 In a small bowl, toss the capers and flour together until the
capers are all coated. Warm up a medium skillet over medium-
high heat and add the oil. When the oil is hot, toss in the
capers and fry them up until they start to look a little golden,
3 to 5 minutes. Some of the caper coating is gonna come off in
the pan, but that's fine. Don't stress. When they look good and
golden to you, pull them out of the pan and put them on a plate
with a paper towel to leach away some of the oil.

2 Store in an airtight jar and they'll last about 5 days.

When you're feelin' sick, you might immediately reach for tomato soup. That's fine, but basic, so maybe consider this shit: parsnips. They've got a bunch of fiber and vitamins, plus this soup is what we can only describe as velvety as fuck.

CREAMY CURRIED PARSNIP SOUP

COOK TIME
45 MIN

>> Makes enough for 4 to 6 people

2 tablespoons olive oil

½ yellow onion, chopped

5 to 6 large parsnips,* peeled and chopped (about 6 cups)

1 medium russet potato, peeled and chopped

5 garlic cloves, chopped

1 tablespoon no-salt curry powder

1 teaspoon ground ginger

½ teaspoon ground cumin

Salt

6 cups vegetable broth

1 cup nondairy milk (we like almond)

¼ cup almonds, walnuts, or macadamia nuts, toasted (see page 46) and chopped up teeny tiny

3 tablespoons minced fresh cilantro

3 tablespoons minced green onions

1 to 2 tablespoons fresh lime juice

Black pepper

1 In a large soup pot, heat the oil over medium-high heat. Add the onion and sauté until it starts lookin' a little golden, about 5 minutes. Add the parsnips and potato and keep stirring that shit around until they start to soften slightly, 3 to 5 minutes. Add the garlic, curry powder, ginger, cumin, and ½ teaspoon salt and sauté for another minute so the spices can kinda wake up and coat those rooty fucks. Add the veggie broth and milk and bring that to a slow simmer. Let that cook till the parsnips and potatoes are soft, at least 30 minutes.

2 While that's cooking, in a small bowl, combine the nuts, cilantro, green onions, and a pinch of salt. Set the crumble aside. LOOK AT YOU MULTITASKING LIKE A MOTHERFUCKER.

3 Once the soup is ready to go you can either: (a) Stick your immersion blender in the pot and let it run until the soup is creamy and your desired level of mild chunks has been achieved. OR (b) Work in batches and puree the soup in a blender until smooth and then pour it back in the pot. Up to you.

4 Once the soup is creamy, stir in the lime juice and taste. Add more salt, lime juice, or some pepper if you want.

5 Serve with the crumble right in the middle of the bowls and maybe put some extra on the table because it's just that good.

* Learn more about these pale motherfuckers on page 244. Can't find them? Sub in celery root instead for a just as fucking delicious soup. Or do 5 cups chopped potatoes, 1 cup carrots. Whatever you got.

LIKE SIPPIN ON A SALAD

Hot weather got you fused with your furniture? Get the fuck up and make some gazpacho. Tomatillos are in season, cheap, low-calorie, and goddamn delicious. And if cold soup isn't your thing on a hot summer day, grab some chips and disguise this as a dip.

TOMATILLO AND CUCUMBER GAZPACHO

1 Grab a big-ass bowl and throw in the cucumbers, tomatillos, tomatoes, peppers, and onion (this could def happen the night before). Then throw one-half to three-quarters of the chopped ingredients into a blender. Add the garlic, oil, both vinegars, the bread, lime juice, cilantro, salt, and cumin to the blender. Now run that shit until it looks pretty smooth in there and pour it back in with the remaining chunks. We like ours on the chunkier side, so we only blend half, but you do you.

2 Let this chill in the fridge for about 1 hour. Garnish and serve. Good for 3 to 4 days in the fridge.

* Is your bread not dried out? Toast that shit in the oven at 325°F until it is. Think about the texture of a crouton. That's what you want.

Got leftovers and tired of cold soup? Add a cup or two of chickpeas or white beans, blend, and make that shit a dip.

COOK TIME
70 MIN

>> **Makes 6 cups, enough for 4 people**

1 English cucumber or 4 Persian cucumbers, chopped (about 2½ cups)

1 pound tomatillos, husked, rinsed, and chopped (about 2½ cups)

1½ cups chopped tomato (about 3 large)

1 cup chopped sweet peppers or bell pepper

1 cup chopped white onion (about ½ onion)

2 garlic cloves, peeled

6 tablespoons olive oil

¼ cup rice vinegar

¼ cup sherry vinegar

2 thick slices day-old* white bread, chopped (about 1½ cups)

Juice of 1 lime

⅓ cup chopped fresh cilantro

½ teaspoon salt

¼ teaspoon ground cumin

Garnish: Cilantro, chopped tomatoes, chopped avocados, or whatever else you've got lying around

>> **Enough for 4 to 6 people who need to warm up**

2 tablespoons olive oil

1 chopped yellow onion

1 large sweet potato, skin on, diced into pieces the size of a penny

1 red bell pepper, chopped

1 jalapeño, minced, optional

2 tablespoons fresh, minced ginger

2 teaspoons ground turmeric*

1 teaspoons dried basil

1 teaspoon paprika

1 tablespoon soy sauce or Bragg Liquid Aminos**

1 (15-ounce) can coconut milk

4 cups veggie broth

1½ cups cooked red beans, black beans, or chickpeas, or 1 (15-ounce) can, rinsed

2 cups chopped kale or other hearty green

2 tablespoons lime juice

Salt and pepper to taste

Between the ginger and turmeric, this will put some fire in you belly. In a good way, though. Not like a burrito belly bomb. Nah, this is more like a stomach sauna. Feels as good as it is good for you.

SWEET POTATO COCONUT SOUP WITH GINGER

1 In a large stockpot, warm up the olive oil over medium heat. Add the onion and sauté it, stirring occasionally, until it starts to look translucent, about 5 minutes. Add the sweet potato, bell pepper, jalapeño (if using), and ginger and cook them for another 5 minutes, stirring occasionally, making sure that the ginger doesn't get burnt. Getting dry in there? Add a tablespoon or two of water and scrape the bottom of the pot.

2 Now add the turmeric, basil, paprika, and soy sauce and keep stirring so that everything gets coated and the spices get a chance to warm up, about 1 minute. Add the coconut milk and broth, cover, and let that shit simmer until the potatoes are tender, about 15 minutes. Stir every couple minutes to make sure that nothing is sticking to the bottom of the pot and that it's only simmering, not fucking boiling.

3 When the potatoes are good to go, fold in the beans, kale, and lime juice and simmer away until the kale wilts and the beans are warm, 3 to 5 more minutes. Taste and add salt, pepper, or whateverthefuck you think it's missing. Serve warm, obviously.

Turmeric is just a ground-up root that looks yellow as fuck. If you can't find it in your store's spice section, scream, then just sub in 1 tablespoon yellow curry powder and leave the rest of the spices out.

*** WTF? See page 180.*

AFTERNOON APPETITE

SNACKS & SIDES

LOS ANGELES, CA

SIDE A

pg.66 – Artichoke Buffalo Dip

pg.67 – Chile-Roasted Broccoli

pg.68 – Swiss Chard Puttanesca

pg.70 – Wine-Braised Artichokes With Fresh Herbs

pg.73 – Fasolakia (Greek Green Beans)

pg.74 – Glazed Bok Choy With Garlic

pg.75 – Roasted Red Bell Pepper And Rosemary Dip

pg.77 – Summertime Carrot Salad

pg.78 – Curtido

pg.79 – Roasted Corn Salsa

pg.81 – Plum Salsa

pg.82 – Stovetop Creamed Collards

SIDE B

pg.83 – Greek Dandelion Greens

pg.84 – Baba Ganoush

pg.85 – Tomato Rice

pg.87 – Figs In A Blanket

pg.88 – Roasted Japanese Sweet Potatoes With Cilantro-Herb Sauce

pg.91 – Pistachio Herb Rice

pg.93 – Oklahoma-Style Fried Okra

pg.95 – Pan-Seared Okra With Lime

pg.96 – Pineapple Fried Rice

pg.97 – Baked Leeks And Parsnips

PRODUCED BY BAD MANNERS

COOK TIME
25 MIN

» **Makes enough for 6 to 8 people**

12 ounces soft silken tofu or white beans, rinsed

½ cup chopped white onion

3 garlic cloves

3 tablespoons apple cider vinegar or white wine vinegar

1 tablespoon rice vinegar

¼ cup olive oil

2 tablespoons minced fresh chives

2 tablespoons minced fresh dill

2 tablespoons minced fresh parsley

½ teaspoon salt

½ teaspoon garlic powder*

2 cans (15 ounces each) artichoke hearts, rinsed and chopped

½ cup Buffalo Sauce (page 210)

½ cup chopped green onions

Corn chips, crackers, or cut-up vegetables, for serving

This St. Louis staple was introduced to us at a potluck and hot damn, it should be a staple of every potluck or game day in America. While traditionally full of chicken, we're using artichoke hearts here and they've never tasted better. And before you ask, yeah this shit can be spicy, so keep some celery on hand.

ARTICHOKE BUFFALO DIP

1 Warm up the oven to 350°F.

2 Throw the tofu, onion, garlic, both vinegars, and the oil into a blender or food processor and run that motherfucker until it looks all smooth. Throw in the fresh herbs, salt, and garlic powder and pulse it a couple of times so everything gets chopped up and mixed in but the herbs are still kinda visible. Transfer to a large bowl.

3 Add the chopped artichoke hearts and Buffalo sauce to the bowl and stir until everything is combined. Pour this spicy son of a bitch into a medium baking dish and stick that shit into the oven for about 15 minutes. You want some of the edges to look golden but not to dry the fucker out.

4 Top with the chopped green onions and serve right away with corn chips, crackers, or vegetables. And yeah, it's spicy. Either you can hang or you can't.

* We know it's weird to call for garlic in two forms, but we have a fucking reason. This helps give it that store-bought ranch taste. Trust us.

This simple side is easy to make and surprisingly delicious. People will ask for the recipe thinking this is some complicated shit. Don't tell them your secrets. Make them earn it.

CHILE-ROASTED BROCCOLI

COOK TIME 25 MIN

》 **Makes enough for 4 as a side**

1 Crank the oven to 450°F.

2 In a large bowl, toss together the broccoli, oil, chile, garlic, and vinegar with a pinch of salt until everything is coated. Spread that fibrous forest out on a baking sheet and roast in the oven until the broccoli is tender and getting a little crispy around some edges, 15 to 20 minutes.

3 Drizzle more vinegar on top of the broccoli if you are feeling it and serve warm.

1 large crown of broccoli,* cut into bite-size little trees

2 tablespoons neutral oil, such as safflower

1 Fresno chile, sliced into rounds

2 garlic cloves, minced

1 tablespoon Fresh Chile Vinegar (page 211) or rice vinegar

Salt

Not a fan of broccoli or just wanna mix it up? Try this with 1½ pounds of green beans instead and reduce the cook time to 8 to 12 minutes. BUT don't sleep on broccoli, that shit's a healthy hero right in your fridge. Learn more on page 224.

>> **Makes enough for 4 as a side**

2 tablespoons olive oil

2 bunches of Swiss chard, cut into ½-inch-wide ribbons, ribs and all*

¼ teaspoon salt

4 to 6 garlic cloves, minced (you do you)

¾ cup dry white wine**

1 tablespoon tomato paste

1 can (14.5 ounces) diced tomatoes

½ to 1 teaspoon red pepper flakes, depending on how cool you are

½ cup sliced pitted Kalamata olives***

¼ cup capers****

1 tablespoon balsamic vinegar

⅓ cup slivered almonds or pine nuts, toasted (see page 46)

Swiss chard is a leafy green from the plant family Chenopodiaceae, which we can't fucking pronounce but encourage you to try. You just need to understand it's related to beets and spinach. Good? Good. Swiss chard is stacked with nutrients, antioxidants, and fiber and is very low in calories. Think of it as your daily multivitamin just in pretty leaf form instead of a chalky pill. Swiss chard grows all over the world and doesn't require much water or light, making it accessible and affordable. Unfortunately, this leafy green gets overlooked by kale-heads and the spinach society, but it's just as versatile as its veggie brethren. You can add it to a smoothie, salad, soup, stew, or sandwich and sauté, stir-fry, or shred it.

SWISS CHARD PUTTANESCA

1 In a large pot, warm up the oil over medium heat. Add the Swiss chard and salt and stir it around so a little oil gets on all of it. Yeah, it might look like way too fucking much chard, but it's gonna cook down, so just keep stirring it for about 5 minutes, until it's all wilted. Add the garlic and wine and cook for another 2 minutes. Mix the tomato paste into the can of diced tomatoes and pour both in, so it's not just a glob. Add the pepper flakes and cook until the chard is cooked all the way down and tastes tender, another 3 to 5 minutes. *DIE CHARD 2: The Cook Down.*

2 Remove from the heat and fold in the olives, capers, and balsamic vinegar. Taste and add more garlic, pepper flakes, whatever you like. Sprinkle the toasted nuts over the top. See? That shit was easy even if you were sipping from the wine bottle the whole time.

3 Serve right away with a glass of that white wine and have yourself one relaxing-ass evening.

* This is roughly 16 cups but will cook WAY DOWN, so calm your shit. You can use rainbow chard or whatever other varieties turn up in your part of town. No stress. And yeah, kale is fine here too.

** If you aren't a wine person, just replace it with veggie broth. Def don't recommend sipping broth from the bottle though.

*** Pitted olives used to be tough to find, but they should be near all that pickled shit in an average grocery store.

**** These pickled sons of bitches are near the olives at the store. They sound all fancy but 1 jar will last you forever and class up your fridge. Get the ones packed in brine, not salt. You fry them all on their own (see page 58), and they will immediately dress up any salad or pasta.

>> **Makes enough for 4 to 6 as a side**

½ cup olive oil

3 large artichokes, cleaned up* and halved lengthwise

1 cup dry white wine**

1 cup vegetable broth

¼ cup minced shallot or white onion

2 garlic cloves, minced

Salt and black pepper

4 tablespoons nondairy butter, cubed

2 tablespoons fresh lemon juice

2 tablespoons minced fresh parsley

2 tablespoons minced fresh chives or mint (or some more parsley, your call)

Panko Pasta Topping (page 205; optional but fucking delicious)

See How to Cook Fresh Artichokes, page 219.

**Out of wine or don't wanna use it? Just replace it with more broth.*

Sure, everyone loves artichokes, but most of y'all dunno how to cook 'em. We're gonna fix that shit right here and now. This recipe is real simple and sounds fancier than it is. This is the kinda shit a restaurant would charge an unreasonable amount of money for on their menu. Now you can dazzle friends and family. Hell, even saying the recipe name sounds like you know what the fuck you're doing.

WINE-BRAISED ARTICHOKES WITH FRESH HERBS

1 In a large saucepan or skillet, warm up the oil over medium heat. Add the artichokes, facedown, and cook until they start looking a little golden brown, about 5 minutes. Add the wine and vegetable broth to the pan. It should come up the sides of the artichokes but not cover them, so don't freak out. Throw in the shallot and garlic and bring this shit to a boil. Now throw on a lid and reduce the heat until the mixture is slowly simmering.

2 Let this whole thing cook until you can pull a leaf out and it tastes all tender, 20 to 30 minutes. Add a splash more wine or broth every now and then if the liquid gets too low in the pan. When they are tender, place the artichokes on a plate and sprinkle them with salt and pepper to taste. Leave the liquid and everything else in the pan.

3 Now we make a pan sauce to really make this shit feel extra fancy. Put the pan back over medium-high heat and get a strong-ass simmer going with the liquid in the pan. Once the liquid has reduced a little, about 5 minutes, add the butter, lemon juice, and a pinch of salt and cook until the sauce looks nice and sorta glossy, another 2 to 3 minutes.

4 Now drizzle that shit over the plated artichokes, sprinkle with the fresh herbs and panko pasta topping (if using). Serve hot and accept tips.

ARTICHOKE ME, DADDY

1 Liquid Courage

2 Fasolakia

3 Baked Eggplant Rice,
page 119

This is a Greek staple in a category of veggie dishes called *lathera* that are all cooked in a generous amount of olive oil. We added potatoes to make this shit a little heartier, but feel free to leave them out and just add more beans. Even though you are familiar with all the ingredients in here, the results are motherfuckin' magic and you've got to make it to find out just how good green beans can actually be. This goes great with our Baked Eggplant Rice (page 119), our Toulatos-Style Stuffed Tomatoes (page 142), or just to replace that tired-ass green bean casserole on Thanksgiving.

FASOLAKIA (GREEK GREEN BEANS)

1 In a medium pot or large, deep sauté pan with a lid, heat the oil over medium-low heat. Add the onions and cook until they start to soften up a little, about 5 minutes. Add the potatoes and garlic and sauté this all for about 3 minutes. Fold in the green beans, oregano, and salt and cook for another minute or two just so all that shit gets warmed up.

2 Pour in the tomato sauce and broth and sprinkle with the mint and parsley. Stir and bring to a simmer. Cover and simmer on low, stirring occasionally, until everything is tender and the liquid has cooked way down, 30 to 40 minutes. Stir in some pepper and a bit of lemon juice, and taste. Add more of whatever you think it needs.

3 Serve warm with some more parsley on top for looks.

*** *Not fucking spaghetti sauce or marinara. Plain tomato sauce in a can, with no seasonings like thyme or basil or whatever. If you get the wrong thing, that shit is on you.*

COOK TIME
50 MIN

>> **Makes enough for 4 as a side**

½ cup olive oil*

1 large yellow or white onion, chopped

4 small golden potatoes, cut into quarter-size chunks

4 garlic cloves, minced

1½ pounds green beans, chopped in half**

1½ teaspoons dried oregano

½ teaspoon salt

1½ cups tomato sauce***

1¼ cups vegetable broth

1 tablespoon minced fresh mint

1 tablespoon minced fresh parsley, plus more for garnish

Black pepper

Juice from ½ a lemon

* *Yeah, it's a lot of oil, but that's how it's done. We've tried scaling it back but this is as low as you can go before the dish tastes totally different.*

** *Learn more on page 236.*

» **Makes enough for 4 to 6 as a side**

½ cup vegetable broth

2 tablespoons tamari or soy sauce

1 tablespoon Fresh Chile Vinegar (page 211) or rice vinegar

2 teaspoons toasted sesame oil

1 teaspoon cornstarch or tapioca flour

2 tablespoons neutral oil, such as safflower or grapeseed

4 heads of baby bok choy, halved lengthwise, or half of one head of bok choy, roughly chopped

4 garlic cloves, minced

1 tablespoon minced fresh ginger

Sesame seeds (optional)

You might be familiar with bok choy, maybe it somehow stumbles onto your plate once or twice a year. But that's not fucking frequently enough. Aside from its slick-ass name, bok choy has a ton of health benefits like folate, vital in the production and repair of DNA. And unlike most other fruits or veggies, bok choy has selenium, which detoxifies the shit out of any cancer-causing agents in your body. It's also fun to pronounce. All around, a solid veggie. 10/10. Would glaze alongside garlic.

GLAZED BOK CHOY WITH GARLIC

1 In a small glass or bowl, mix together the broth, tamari, vinegar, and sesame oil. Whisk in the cornstarch and make sure it's not all clumpy. Set aside.

2 Heat up a large skillet over medium-high heat and add 1 tablespoon of the neutral oil. Put the bok choy in the pan in a single layer, cut-side down, and cook those leafy bastards, without moving them, until they start to brown a little underneath, 2 to 3 minutes. Flip and do the same shit on the other side.

3 Take the boy choy out when they look good and lightly browned and put them on plate. Add the remaining 1 tablespoon neutral oil to the pan and keep cooking 'cause this shit ain't over yet. Throw in the garlic and ginger and cook for about 30 seconds, just until it starts smelling good. Whisk in the broth mixture and simmer until the cornstarch starts to thicken the sauce up and make it look a little glossy, 30 to 60 seconds.

4 Return the bok choy back to the pan and cook, flipping it over at least once, until everything is covered with the sauce. Sprinkle with the sesame seeds (if using) and serve immediately.

Even if you don't have much confidence in the kitchen, everyone can make a dip. Especially when roasting bell peppers, you'll look like you know what the fuck you're doing. Outside of standard dip duty, you can spread this on a sandwich or slice some cucumber up and BAM! you have a gluten-free snack. Plus there's a ton of protein in there for all you weirdos who give a shit about that kinda thing. Y'all prob buy deodorant with protein in it, too, huh?

ROASTED BELL PEPPER AND ROSEMARY DIP

1 In a medium skillet, warm up 1 tablespoon of the olive oil over medium heat. Add the onion and a pinch of salt and sauté that shit until the onion starts to get some color on it, about 5 minutes. Add the rosemary and garlic and cook for another minute or so, just so the garlic isn't all raw anymore. Remove from the heat.

2 In a food processor or blender, throw in the beans, roasted peppers, vinegar, almond butter, lemon juice, smoked paprika, ½ teaspoon salt, the cooked onion mixture, and the remaining 1 tablespoon olive oil. Let that shit run until everything looks mostly smooth and relatively creamy.

3 Serve right away with some crackers, crostini, or bread or let it chill in the fridge for a while to thicken up. It will keep in the fridge for about 1 week.

* Never roasted a bell pepper? Shit's easy. Flip to page 223 and we'll walk you thru it.

** It's also great on a sandwich with our Smoky Tempeh Slices (page 204) and is essential in our Figs in a Blanket (page 87).

COOK TIME

12 MIN

» **Makes about 2 cups**

2 tablespoons olive oil

½ yellow onion, chopped

Salt

2 tablespoons chopped fresh rosemary

2 garlic cloves, chopped

1½ cups cooked cannellini or white beans or 1 can (15 ounces), drained and rinsed

2 roasted red bell peppers*

2 tablespoons sherry or red wine vinegar

2 tablespoons almond butter or tahini

1 tablespoon fresh lemon juice

2 tablespoons smoked paprika

Crackers or bread, for serving**

Lots of hippie restaurants have something like this on their menus but list it as some fake-ass tuna salad. That's an insult to carrots. Serve the salad chilled, as a dip with some chips or crackers, as the filling for some lettuce cups, or slather it between 2 slices of toasted sourdough bread with some lettuce for a bomb-as-hell sandwich. Learn more about carrots as a low-key super food on page 226.

SUMMERTIME CARROT SALAD

Throw everything together in a large bowl and mix that shit up until everything is incorporated. Let it sit in the fridge for at least 1 hour before serving so all the flavors get mixed together and it gets a chance to chill.

WTF? See page 180.

COOK TIME
65 MIN

>> Makes enough for 4 to 6 as a side

4 cups shredded carrots, as small as you can get them

1 cup chopped green onions

1 red bell pepper, diced

½ cup chopped fresh cilantro

½ cup mashed avocado, plain hummus, or your favorite nondairy mayo

½ cup apple cider vinegar or rice vinegar

¼ cup agave or your favorite liquid sweetener

2 tablespoons Bragg Liquid Aminos*

1 tablespoon celery seeds

Wanna add some protein to this shit? Sub in 2 cups of cooked red lentils for 2 cups of the shredded carrots. That's gonna turn this from a side into a filling as hell lunch.

›› Makes about 4 cups

1 head of green cabbage*

2 carrots, grated (about 1 cup)

1 white onion, thinly sliced

1 to 2 jalapeños, chopped

2 teaspoons dried oregano

2 teaspoons salt

2½ cups white vinegar

1 cup water

* Learn more about the miracle that is cabbage on page 225.

Curtido, aka Salvadoran slaw, is kinda like sauerkraut or kimchi in that it's cabbage with a bunch of veggies. There's a little pickling going on here, so be prepared to let this shit sit for a bit, at least an hour. But the longer you let it marinate, the more flavor you're gonna get. Ideally you'll pair this with pupusas (see Jackfruit Pupusas, page 132), but it's great on tacos, salads, anything you might put slaw on.

CURTIDO

1 Thinly slice the cabbage and place it in a large bowl. Just think coleslaw and it'll be fine. You should end up with about 10 cups. Fold in the carrots, onion, jalapeño, and oregano. Sprinkle with the salt and kinda smush everything together. Very technical terms right here. You want to use the salt to help rough up the cabbage so it will soften up better in the vinegar. Do this for a minute or two, making sure to mix everything up while you smush.

2 Add the vinegar and water to the cabbage mixture and toss everything together. Fill a large jar or container with the cabbage mixture, pressing down tight to get as much in there as you can, and then top it off with the brine. You didn't realize you'd made a brine, huh? See, cooking isn't tough. The terms are just fucking weird.

3 Put on the lid and stick that shit in the fridge for at least 2 hours but preferably overnight. Serve with pupusas or eat it straight from the damn jar.

4 This will keep in your fridge for at least 2 weeks.

You don't hafta go to a taqueria to enjoy this shit. It's as versatile as it is delicious. No chips? No problem. Serve it in lettuce cups, wrap it in a tortilla, or just eat it with a spoon and call it a fuckin day. Cheat on tomato salsa, come on. We won't tell.

ROASTED CORN SALSA

1 Get your grill (or grill pan) nice and hot. Brush the corn with a little oil just so that they don't stick to the grill, then throw them on there. Corn is edible raw so all we're really doing here is lookin' for char marks so we get some of that smoky flavor in the salsa. Turn the corn to another side every couple minutes or so until all the ears are charred to your liking. Remove from the heat and let the corn cool while you chop up everything else.

2 In a big bowl, mix together the cucumber, tomato, red onion, chiles, and cilantro. Cut the roasted corn right off the cob and toss it in; you should get 3 to 4 cups. Add the lime juice and salt and stir so all the flavors get mixed up. Serve right away or let it chill in the fridge.

3 Keeps for about 3 to 4 days.

COOK TIME
25 MIN

》 **Makes enough for 6 to 8 at a party**

4 ears corn, all shucked and naked

Oil

1 cup chopped Persian or English cucumber

1 cup chopped tomato

1 cup chopped red onion

1 to 2 Fresno chiles or jalapeño peppers, minced

½ cup chopped fresh cilantro

½ cup fresh lime juice (4 to 5 limes)

½ teaspoon salt

1 Plum Salsa

2 Roasted Corn Salsa, page 79

Oh, you think a fruit salsa is weird? Well guess what, asshole? TOMATOES ARE A FRUIT, TOO. So unclench your ass and enjoy this fruit-flavor explosion.

PLUM SALSA

>> **Makes about 4 cups**

1 In a large bowl, mix everything together and let it sit for about 5 minutes. Taste with a chip or whateverthefuck you plan on serving it with and see if you need more lime juice or anything like that. Naw? Then get that shit on the table.

2 If you're making it the night before, leave the avocado out until you're about to serve it. The salsa should last about 3 days in the fridge.

Can't find plums? You can use nectarines, peaches, or pluots here. All would be fucking delicious.

3 cups chopped red or black plums (about 6)*

½ red onion, chopped (about 1 cup)

½ cup chopped fresh cilantro

1 clove garlic, minced

1 jalapeño, minced

¼ cup fresh lime juice (2 to 3 limes)

1½ cups chopped avocado (about 1 avocado)

½ teaspoon salt

COOK TIME
45 MIN

»Makes enough for 4 people

Salt

2 large bunches of collard greens,* thick stems and ribs removed, leaves cut into ½-inch strips (about 10 cups)

2 tablespoons olive oil

3 large shallots or ½ white onion, finely chopped

2 garlic cloves, minced

3 tablespoons all-purpose flour

2 teaspoons smoked paprika

2 cups nondairy milk, such as oat or almond

Black pepper

Juice of ½ lemon

This is our take on the Thanksgiving staple creamed spinach, which is usually overcooked, watery, and flavorless but NOT. OUR. SHIT. Collards hold up much better and your whole family will be glad you took over side-dish duty from your aunt this year.

STOVETOP CREAMED COLLARDS

1 Find a large bowl and fill it with some ice water and set it aside. Grab a big-ass pot and fill it with water and a big pinch of salt. Bring to a boil over medium-high heat and throw in the collards. Cook until they're bright green and beginning to soften, 3 to 4 minutes. Stick the leaves into the ice water bowl from earlier to cool. Yeah, that's right, we blanched that shit. Look at you cook. After the leaves have cooled, squeeze the water out as best you can without being a lunatic about it. Set them aside on your cutting board or somewhere not in your way.

2 In a large soup pot (like the one from earlier), warm up the oil over medium heat. Add the shallots and sauté until they start to look golden, about 5 minutes. Add the garlic, flour, and smoked paprika and stir for about 1 minute. Whisk in the milk, making sure there are no chunks, and bring to a simmer, whisking often for about 2 minutes until you can feel the mixture start to thicken up. Fold in the drained collards, add a pinch each of salt and pepper and reduce the heat to medium-low. Simmer, stirring often, until the greens are extra tender and the sauce thickens, about 15 minutes. Drizzle the lemon juice on top and add more salt and pepper if you think the collards need it. Serve warm.

* Not into collards or can't find them? Sub in another sturdy green like kale. Yeah, sturdy.

Yeah, that's right. That weed growing in your yard is not only edible but tasty as hell. But we recommend picking them up at the store because those haven't been pissed on by your neighbor's dog. These makes an excellent meal with our Stuffed Tomatoes (page 142) or Baked Eggplant Rice (page 119).

GREEK DANDELION GREENS

》Makes enough for 4 people

Salt

2 bunches of dandelion greens,* chopped (about 8 cups)

3 tablespoons olive oil

1 clove garlic, minced (optional)**

1½ teaspoons grated lemon zest

2 tablespoons fresh lemon juice

Black pepper

1 Fill a large pot with salted water and bring to a boil over medium-high heat. Add the dandelion greens and reduce the heat to a simmer. Cook until the greens have softened up and mellowed out in taste, 5 to 8 minutes. Scoop out 1 cup of the cooking liquid and put it aside. Drain the rest of the liquids, leaving the greens in the colander for a sec.

2 Add the oil to the pot you just used and put it over medium heat. Throw in the garlic (if using) and stir that shit around for 30 seconds. Toss in the drained greens, lemon zest, lemon juice, ¼ teaspoon salt, and the cup of cooking liquid you saved earlier. Let everything warm up for about 3 minutes while you stir, and add some black pepper or more salt if you're feeling it.

3 Serve right away.

* It's a damn shame how much dandelion greens are ignored. They're fucking delicious. If you can't find them, sub in spinach, chard, sweet potato leaves, whatever kinda soft edible greens you can get your hands on.

** Optional but IT'S GARLIC, SO HOW DO YOU NOT?

>> Makes enough
for 4 to snack on

1 large eggplant*
(about 2½ pounds)

¼ cup tahini**

2 tablespoons olive oil

2 tablespoons fresh
lemon juice

2 to 3 garlic cloves,
chopped

1 teaspoons ground
cumin

½ teaspoon salt

2 tablespoons
chopped fresh parsley

* Learn more about this
weird-ass veggie on
page 233.

** What in the fuck is
tahini? It's a paste made
from sesame seeds and
used for tons of badass
dishes. Think peanut
butter but with sesame
seeds.

In late summer, eggplant is everywhere and you can buy 'em real cheap. This makes a solid summer dip that's smoky enough to pair with just about anything else you're pulling off the grill.

BABA GANOUSH

1 First you need to roast the fucking eggplant. You can do this shit one of two ways. (Either way, be sure to stab the eggplant with a fork a couple times before you cook it so the steam escapes without that purple fucker falling apart on you.)

OPTION 1: GRILL
You can grill the whole motherfucker on a grill preheated to 300°F. Rotate it occasionally until all the sides are black and it starts collapsing in on itself like a deflated football. This will take 25 to 30 minutes.

OPTION 2: ROAST
Preheat the oven to 375°F. Put your eggplant on a baking sheet and roast it whole until you can poke a knife through it like soft butter, 20 to 30 minutes.

2 When the eggplant has cooled down a bit, about 15 minutes, cut that shit in half. Scoop out all the flesh using a spoon and toss it right into a food processor or blender, leaving the skin behind to think about what it did impersonating Grimace like that. Add all the rest of the ingredients except the parsley and run that fucking machine until the eggplant looks nice and smooth, about a minute. Throw in the parsley and run the machine for a couple extra seconds. If you like your dips a little chunky, you could skip the food processor and just mash all of this shit around in a bowl with a fork. Just chop the garlic smaller if you're not using the food processor.

3 Taste the dip and add more of whateverthefuck you think it needs. More lemon? More garlic? More cumin? Do whatever. Serve it warm or cold. It keeps in the fridge for at least 5 days.

This is the ideal basic rice recipe you should have on deck. Tomato rice is great just to have in the fridge if you're doing meal prep or anything for the week.

TOMATO RICE

1 Grab a large soup pot with a lid and heat the oil over medium-high heat. Throw in the onion and chile and stir them around until the onion starts to look translucent, about 3 minutes. Add the cumin seeds and cook for a minute more. Now stir in the bay leaf, garlic, tomatoes, salt, coriander, and chili powder. Your place should smell so fucking good right now that we're jealous just thinking about it. Cook this mess up until the tomatoes start to break down, another 5 to 7 minutes. Then fold in the rice. Cook for another 30 seconds just to get the rice all mixed up, then pour in the veggie broth.

2 Now let that shit come to a simmer. Once it's there, reduce the heat to low, give it a quick stir, then throw on the lid. Let that shit go for 15 to 20 minutes. Don't even think about checking on it before 15 minutes. Once the rice is fluffy and has absorbed almost all the broth it's good to go. Remove from the heat and fold in the lime juice and cilantro and fluff that fucker with a fork. Serve right away. It keeps in the fridge for about a week.

COOK TIME 50 MIN

》 **Makes enough for 4 people**

2 tablespoons grapeseed or other neutral oil

1 medium onion, chopped (about 2 cups)

1 jalapeño or serrano chile, chopped

1 teaspoon cumin seeds

1 bay leaf

3 garlic cloves, chopped

8 medium tomatoes, chopped (about 3 cups)

½ teaspoon salt

1 teaspoon ground coriander or cumin

½ teaspoon chili powder

2 cups basmati rice, rinsed

2½ cups vegetable broth or water

Juice of 1 lime (about 1 tablespoon)

1 cup chopped fresh cilantro

STUFFED FOR YOUR PLEASURE

DON'T BE WEIRD ABOUT IT

This might be the classiest recipe in this fucker and it's basically a sleepover staple all grown up. Don't be scared of figs; they're one of humanity's oldest snacks and you deserve a fancy plate of food now and then. Go ahead and treat yourself. Learn more about these ancient fucks on page 234.

FIGS IN A BLANKET

1 Crank the oven to 400°F. Line a large baking sheet with some parchment paper.

2 Grab your sheet of puff pastry and roll it on a lightly floured surface to a 12 × 6-inch rectangle. Cut lengthwise into 1-inch-wide strips and then cut those up into 4 pieces about 3 inches long. You know, like 24 little 1 × 3-inch strips that you can wrap up the figs. Don't freak the fuck out just 'cause we wrote down some numbers.

3 Scoop out about 1 teaspoon or more of the bell pepper and rosemary dip and press into a fig half, into the side that has the hole in the center. Place the fig half in the center of one pastry strip. Brush one end of the pastry with some of that nondairy milk, wrap that fig up, and press the ends of the pastry shut. We like to try to tuck the ends under the figs when we put them on the baking sheet so those figs stay tucked in their damn blankets as they bake. Keep stuffing and tucking until you're all out of figs.

4 Brush the top of each pastry with the rest of the milk and sprinkle with some poppy seeds. Bake these fucking adorable apps until the pastry looks golden brown and, well, puffed, 8 to 12 minutes. Let them cool slightly before serving.

COOK TIME
45 MIN

» **Makes about 24**

1 sheet frozen puff pastry,* thawed but still cold

12 fresh figs, halved lengthwise**

1 cup Roasted Bell Pepper and Rosemary Dip (page 75)

2 tablespoons nondairy milk

2 tablespoons poppy seeds***

This should be near the frozen pie crust in the store.

***You can use dried, whole figs here. Just soak them in some warm water for 30 minutes before you start so they kinda rehydrate and are easier to work with.*

****You could def sub in an everything bagel seasoning blend or sesame seeds here. It's basically just for looks.*

COOK TIME
75 MIN

>> **Makes enough for 4 to 8 people**

SWEET POTATOES

4 Japanese sweet potatoes, unpeeled, scrubbed clean*

Extra virgin olive oil, for drizzling

Salt

CILANTRO-HERB SAUCE

2 cups chopped cilantro leaves and stems

1 cup fresh mint leaves

½ cup chopped green onions

1-inch piece fresh ginger, roughly chopped

1 jalapeño (optional), chopped

¼ cup fresh lemon juice (1 to 2 lemons)

2 tablespoons rice vinegar

½ teaspoon salt

2 tablespoons olive, avocado, or grapeseed oil

Japanese sweet potatoes have a fluffier texture than regular sweet potatoes but all of the taste, so honestly, it's time we just switch over to this superior spud. This dish is fucking awesome all by itself but makes a great bowl alongside any of our tofu or jackfruit recipes and any kind of greens or slaw.

ROASTED JAPANESE SWEET POTATOES WITH CILANTRO-HERB SAUCE

1 Crank the oven to 400°F. Line a baking sheet with parchment paper.

2 Prick each sweet potato all over with a fork, oil up their skins, and sprinkle all over with salt. Stick these delicious spuds on the lined pan and roast until they're tender, about 1 hour depending on how big they are. After 1 hour, poke one with a sharp knife. Finding no resistance? You are good to go.

3 While those are roasting, make the cilantro-herb sauce: Throw the cilantro, mint, green onions, ginger, jalapeño (if using), lemon juice, vinegar, and salt in a blender or food processor and run that shit until a kinda paste/sauce hybrid comes together. With it running, pour in the oil so it gets all mixed it. Looking too thick? Add a tablespoon of water. Done.

4 When everything is ready, split open the potatoes and drizzle the sauce on top. While we could legit eat just these potatoes alone, these go with almost everything and we never ever get tired of these sweet fucks.

* They reheat fucking perfectly so even if you're dining alone don't roast just one. Might as well do at least four since it's hardly any extra work.

ALMOST AS SWEET & SPICY AS YOU

1 Pomegranate Cola Jackfruit, page 120

2 Pistachio Herb Rice

3 Pomegranate Seeds (see page 244)

We whipped this up for our friends Mick and Roxy's wedding so if it was good enough for that, it's def good enough for you to eat over your laptop in the dark. Serve it warm or at room temp alongside our Pomegranate Cola Jackfruit (page 120) for all the flavors of takeout without having to bring any strangers into your building.

PISTACHIO HERB RICE

1 Put the saffron in the bottom of a small glass and pour in the hot water. Set that shit aside while you cook the rice.

2 Grab a large pot with a lid and warm up the oil over medium-high heat. Add the rice and salt and sauté around for about 2 minutes so that all the rice can get coated in oil and a little toasty. Stir in the water and bring to a boil. Reduce the heat to low and throw on the lid. Let this cook until all the water has been adsorbed and the rice is fluffy, about 15 minutes. You know how the fuck rice should look.

3 When the rice looks good, pour that saffron water over one-quarter of the pot, fishing out the threads, cover, and let that shit sit for another 10 minutes so that the rice can get a good dye job. (Not using the saffron? Skip to the next step.)

4 Scoop the rice into a large bowl and fluff it with a fork. Try to keep the saffron-colored rice and the white rice fluffed separately in that same bowl until right at the end so the colors don't get all fucked up. We want this shit pretty, ok?

* Saffron can be fucking expensive, so if you don't wanna buy it, don't stress. It's in here 75 percent for looks anyway.

** No pistachios? Toasted walnut, almonds, or pumpkin seeds would all be legit here too. Use what you got.

COOK TIME
40 MIN

» **Makes enough for 4 to 6 people**

Pinch of saffron threads*

3 tablespoons hot water

3 tablespoons olive oil

2 cups basmati or other long grain white rice, rinsed

½ teaspoon salt

3½ cups water or vegetable broth

½ cup chopped dried fruit, such as cherries, apricots, cranberries, or a mix, plus more for garnish

3 tablespoons each (or at least 2 of them) chopped fresh dill, tarragon, cilantro, and/or mint

½ cup chopped pistachios, plus more for garnish**

Juice from 1 lemon

Salt and black pepper

(continued)

5 Fold in the fruit, herbs, and pistachios. Now gently mix all the rice together. Drizzle the lemon juice on top and taste. Add salt and pepper, and more of whateverthefuck you want.

6 Serve warm or at room temperature with more nuts and herbs on top so it looks extra sexy. This dish is perfect to bring to someone's house (are we doing that yet?) because it looks impressive as fuck and can be served at room temperature but is easy as fuck to make and they'll never know.

We grew up eating fried okra but discovered when we got out in the world that not everyone knows what the fuck they're doing when it comes to this Southern staple. Too many people over-bread these bitches and they come out thick, heavy, and like lil slimy okra corndogs. WRONG. You want 'em just dusted with flour and cornmeal so they get crispy, not coated. This is the Oklahoma way—the only way to do it. Trust us. Don't trust okra? Get educated on page 243.

COOK TIME
20 MIN

》 **Makes enough for 2 to 4 people**

¾ cup cornmeal

½ cup all-purpose flour

½ tablespoon salt

¼ teaspoon black pepper

Peanut oil, for frying

3 cups sliced fresh or frozen okra (¼ inch thick or smaller)

OKLAHOMA-STYLE FRIED OKRA

1 In a shallow bowl, mix the cornmeal, flour, salt, and pepper together.

2 Pour about ½ inch of oil into a large skillet and set over medium-high heat to get hot.

3 Toss the sliced okra in the cornmeal mix, making sure all those slimy fuckers get coated. When the oil is hot, put the coated okra in the skillet, leaving behind all the flour you didn't use. Fry those green fucks around until nice and brown, 8 to 12 minutes.

4 Place them on a plate to cool down for a sec, but serve hot.

1 Sticky Tofu with
Sweet Sesame Sauce,
page 135, on rice

2 Pan-Seared Okra
with Lime

Okra season is during summer, usually between June and September, and we are always stoked when it starts showing up in stores. It thrives in hot, humid climates, making it a staple of Southern cooking. It looks kinda like a geometric pepper and is usually green, but there are burgundy-colored variations—fuckers taste the exact same but look fancy. Okra's also got a shitload of vitamin C and fiber, so it's as healthy as it is delicious. It's a versatile veggie and a great addition to almost any dish, but most of the time we just cook this shit up as a solo snack.

PAN-SEARED OKRA WITH LIME

》Makes enough for 4 as a side

1 tablespoon olive oil

1½ pounds small okra pods*

½ cup diced shallots or red onion

1 tablespoon tamari or soy sauce

Juice of 2 limes (about ¼ cup)

Pinch of salt

Sesame seeds, for serving

Cilantro, for serving

1 Warm up a large skillet over medium-high heat and add the oil. Once everything is warmed, throw in the okra and try to make it an even layer so all that shit is cooking at the same time. Toss it around a couple of times, then let it sit for at least 10 to 15 seconds between tosses to start seeing some good sear marks on the okra. This should all take about 3 minutes. Ya don't want these bitches gettin' all soggy and limp, just browned in some spots on the outside without getting all overcooked and mushy. See here, some people whine about okra being "slimy" and that means it's been overcooked. Blame the kitchen, not the veggie.

2 Add the shallots, toss them around, then drizzle in the tamari. Cook this until the shallots get translucent, another 2 minutes. Add the lime juice and cook for another 30 seconds, then remove from the heat. Sprinkle in the salt. Serve topped with sesame seeds and cilantro.

You wanna get the smallest okra possible 'cause it'll be the least tough and we are tryin' to not cook this shit that long. Learn more on page 243.

≫ **Makes enough for 4 people**

2 teaspoons neutral-tasting oil like safflower

4 cups cooked leftover short grain white or brown rice

1 carrot, chopped

½ yellow onion, chopped

1 cup frozen green peas

1 cup chopped fresh or defrosted frozen pineapple

2 garlic cloves, minced

2 tablespoons soy sauce or tamari

1 tablespoon water

1 tablespoon rice vinegar

1 teaspoon chili paste or an Asian-style hot sauce like Sriracha

2 cup chopped-up greens like spinach*

½ cup sliced green onions

The trick to good fried rice is to use cold leftover cooked rice. Don't use freshly cooked rice because it'll get all mushy and that shit just won't work. Fry like you know what the fuck you're doing.

PINEAPPLE FRIED RICE

1 In a large wok or skillet, warm 1 teaspoon of the oil over medium heat. Add the carrot and onions and cook until the onions are translucent, about 3 minutes. Add the frozen peas, pineapple, and garlic, mix well, and cook for another 3 minutes so the peas defrost and the pineapple warms the fuck up. Remove all the vegetables from the pan and scrape the pan clean 'cause we aren't fucking done.

2 In a small glass, mix together the soy sauce, water, vinegar, and chili paste. Heat the wok back up over medium heat and add the remaining 1 teaspoon oil. Throw in the cold rice and stir-fry until it begins to warm, 3 to 5 minutes. Drizzle the sauce over the rice, mix well, and add the cooked vegetables and spinach. Stir-fry for a minute or two so everything is well mixed and the spinach has wilted. Fold in the green onions. Turn off the heat. Serve immediately.

Fresh or frozen spinach works here, but fresh is best if you've got it.

This simple side dish is perfect when you need a little extra something on the dinner table but you wanna put in almost no effort. You can stick this shit in the oven and move on to your main dish without looking back. It's not fussy and people love anything baked. Can't find parsnips? Fuck it, use carrots. See? Not fussy at all. But you can learn more about those pale fuckers on page 244.

BAKED LEEKS AND PARSNIPS

1 Crank the oven to 425°F.

2 Grab a large baking dish. Throw in the leeks, parsnips, oil, garlic, rosemary, and salt and toss it all around the baking dish until all that shit is coated. Add the veggie broth and cover the dish with foil.

3 Throw it in the oven for 20 minutes. After 20 minutes, remove the foil, stir, then roast again until everything is tender, 10 to 15 more minutes.

4 Drizzle the lemon juice on top and serve hot or at room temperature.

COOK TIME
40 MIN

>> **Makes enough for 4 people**

3 leeks, pale green and white parts only, halved lengthwise

5 parsnips (or carrots if you hate adventure), halved lengthwise

2 tablespoons olive oil

3 garlic cloves, thinly sliced

2 teaspoons chopped fresh rosemary

½ teaspoon salt

½ cup vegetable broth

1 tablespoon fresh lemon juice

FEAST DE RESISTANCE

MENU

Pear, Tempeh, and
Arugula Sandwich
100

Broccoli Rabe Pasta
103

Beeteroni Pizza
104

Orange Peel Cauliflower
107

Basil Pesto Summer Salad
with Sunflower Seeds
109

Nashville Hot Shroom
Sammie
110

Caramelized Fennel
Tarts
113

Teriyaki Jackfruit with
Curry Udon Noodles
117

Baked Eggplant Rice
119

Pomegranate Cola
Jackfruit
120

How to Bake Tofu
121

Lemongrass Baked Tofu
122

Ginger-Turmeric Tofu
Marinade
123

Chipotle Pumpkin
Tamales
124

Grilled Nectarine Soba
Noodles
127

Shroom Asada
128

Jackfruit Pupusas
132

Sticky Tofu with Sweet
Sesame Sauce
135

Coconut Green Curry
with Avocado
137

Summer Tomato Tart
139

Zucchini Blossom Pasta
140

Toulatos-Style Stuffed
Tomatoes or Bell
Peppers
142

Simple Sesame Noodles
with Edamame and
Watercress
144

COOK TIME

15 MIN

》 **Makes enough
for 4 sandwiches**

2 tablespoons olive
oil, plus more as
needed

8 slices whole-grain
or sourdough bread

Whole-grain or
regular Dijon mustard

1 batch Pickled Red
Onions (page 195) or
½ red onion, sliced
into rounds

2 red Anjou or Bosc
pears, sliced

1 batch cashew
cheese sauce
(page 213)

2 cups arugula*

1 batch of Smoky
Tempeh Slices
(page 204)

So this is one of those recipes that isn't really
a recipe so much as a way to put a couple recipes
in this book together to make a fucking delicious
meal. And trust us, it's worth the effort.

PEAR, TEMPEH, AND ARUGULA SANDWICH

1 In a large skillet or frying pan, warm up the olive oil over
medium heat. Add the slices of bread, making sure they all get
a little oil on them, and toast those fuckers on both sides until
they're golden brown. You might need to do this shit in batches
depending on the size of your pan, and in that case you'll need
some more oil.

2 Once the bread is toasted, it's time to build the sammie. On
one slice of toasted bread, spread a good helping of mustard
then pile on the pickled red onions. Add the pear slices and
make sure that this all seems to be at an even level. Don't
make this shit messier than it needs to be. On the other slice
of toasted bread, smear a good helping of the cashew cheese,
then add ¼ cup of the arugula, then a couple slices of the
tempeh. Press this slice on top of the other slice and cut the
sandwich in half while pressing. Now enjoy the best sammie
you've had in a long-ass time.

** No arugula? Spinach, mixed greens, or whatever lettuce you've got works
fine here.*

IF DA VINCI HAD BEEN A
SANDWICH ARTIST

NEW SUPPER STAPLE JUST DROPPED

This is a pretty basic dish and solid starting place if you're just trying to master a few recipes. This sounds fancier than it is and comes together quick. Also don't ever order this shit at a restaurant. They'll def put it on the menu for people who don't know any better but it's like ordering peanut butter and jelly or, worse, pancakes. C'mon, y'all, just light your money on fire then.

BROCCOLI RABE PASTA

1 Cook the pasta according to the package directions. Scoop out ½ cup of the cooking water and save, then drain the pasta.

2 In a large sauté pan or skillet, heat 2 tablespoons of the olive oil over medium-high heat. Add the broccoli rabe and a pinch of salt and sauté until the stalks are all tender and, you know, edible. Add 3 tablespoons of the olive oil, the garlic, and pepper flakes and sauté for about 1 minute, or until the garlic doesn't look so raw. Add ¼ cup of the reserved pasta water and the cooked pasta and toss that shit together until everything is mixed up. Drizzle with the lemon juice and ¼ teaspoon salt and toss again.

3 If it's looking a little dry, add the rest of the pasta water and about another 1 tablespoon olive oil. Top with the panko and serve right away.

COOK TIME 25 MIN

>> **Makes enough for 4 people**

16 ounces of your favorite medium pasta, like fusilli or trofie, uncooked

5 to 6 tablespoons olive oil

1 pound broccoli rabe or regular broccoli, roughly chopped into 2-inch bites*

Salt

4 garlic cloves, minced

½ teaspoon red pepper flakes

Juice of ½ lemon

1 cup Panko Pasta Topping (page 205)

* Learn more about all kinds of badass broccoli on page 224.

COOK TIME 40 MIN

>> **Makes 4 individual Pizzas**

1 batch Everyday Pizza Dough (page 198)

Cornmeal, for dusting

TOPPINGS

House Marinara (page 197)

Cashew Cheese Sauce (page 213)

Beeteroni, sliced (page 200)

Olive oil, for brushing the crust

Pantry Parm (page 199)

Hot sauce, for serving

We weren't gonna just give you a beeteroni recipe without taking you all the way to the net. Here's the pizza you've been missing without any of the mystery meat but all of the flavor. We'll be accepting slices if you feel like saying thanks. Learn more about beets and why they're fucking amazing on page 222.

BEETERONI PIZZA

1 Make the pizza dough on page 198 through step 4. Start cranking up the oven to 475°F.

2 Roll out one ball of the dough using the instructions on page 199. Move it over to a baking sheet dusted with some cornmeal and let's get toppin. Spread about ½ cup of the house marinara over your dough, leaving about 1 inch around the edges as the crust. You know how the fuck a pizza should look. Drizzle at least ⅓ cup cashew cheese sauce, over the top, then toss on the cooked beeteroni slices. Repeat that shit with the remaining dough until you got four pizzas ready to fucking go.

3 Brush the crusts with olive oil and bake until the crusts look golden, 10 to 12 minutes. Grab that pantry parm and sprinkle some of that shit on top before serving.

4 Serve hot, with some hot sauce on the side if you like a little fire on your 'za.

❶ Pantry Parm,
page 199

1 Glazed Bok Choy with Garlic, page 74

2 Orange Peel Cauliflower

Ya like General Tso's chicken? Or you've definitely had orange chicken. Well, that's the kinda shit we're aimin' for here. Also, not a thing in China. That is some specifically American shit. There's even a whole documentary about how American-Chinese food was designed for white American palates by immigrants. See, in the 1880s America had this fucked-up law called the Chinese Exclusion Act that prevented immigrants from holding jobs at American companies. So a shitload of Chinese restaurants start popping up. And the dude who created the original dish? Taiwanese. General Tso's Chicken has absolutely nothing the fuck to do with China or General Zuo Zongtang. Which, by the way, his successful military career aside, General Zuo was really into growing his own food. Zuo tried to reform commercial agriculture, believing it'd strengthen China's self-sufficiency and improve the standard of living for communities. Anyway, that's the kinda shit we're aiming for here.

ORANGE PEEL CAULIFLOWER

1 First, we gotta get the cauliflower ready. Warm your oven up to 450°F and lightly grease a rimmed baking sheet. Chop up your cauliflower into little trees no bigger than your thumb. That's right, tiny-ass little trees. Whisk together the flour, cornstarch, garlic powder, ground ginger, salt, water, and oil in a big bowl until a batter forms with no chunks. Toss in the cauliflower and mix it around until all the pieces look a little coated. Spread the cauliflower out on the baking sheet, keeping any extra batter in the bowl, and roast for 15 to 20 minutes or until it starts looking golden in there.

COOK TIME
45 MIN

>> **Makes enough for 4 people**

CAULIFLOWER

1 head of cauliflower

½ cup rice flour or all-purpose flour

3 tablespoons cornstarch

½ teaspoon garlic powder

½ teaspoon ground ginger

¼ teaspoon salt

⅔ cup water

1 tablespoon neutral oil like safflower

ORANGE SAUCE

1 tablespoons neutral oil like safflower

1 tablespoon minced or grated fresh ginger

4 garlic cloves, minced

¼ cup soy sauce or tamari

3 tablespoons rice vinegar

3 tablespoons brown sugar

1 tablespoon pure maple syrup

(continued)

1 tablespoon Sriracha or your favorite hot sauce

2 tablespoons tomato paste

Zest from 1 orange

1 tablespoon cornstarch

¼ cup cold water

Green onions and sesame seeds, for serving

2 While the cauliflower is getting it's roast on, make the sauce. In a medium saucepan, warm the oil over medium heat. Add the fresh ginger and garlic to the pot and saute them for 30 seconds. Just enough time to wake up those flavors but not enough time to burn the shit out of the garlic. Add the soy sauce, vinegar, brown sugar, maple syrup, sriracha, tomato paste, and half of the orange zest and whisk that shit together until there aren't any chunks. Bring to simmer for about 3 minutes or until the sauce thickens.

3 In a small glass mix together the cornstarch and water until it's all combined. Now whisk this into the simmering pot and let it cook for another minute. You'll see this shit start thickening up fast, but you don't want it any thicker than a good gravy. We still got to coat the cauliflower, you know? Turn off the heat when it's looking right.

4 When 15 to 20 minutes in the oven have passed, dump the cauliflower back in a big bowl and pour the mixture from the stovetop on top. Make sure everything is coated. Drop those motherfuckers back on the baking sheet, leaving any extra sauce in the bowl, and roast for another 5 to 8 minutes, just so everything is warm and the cauliflower can get a little crispy again.

5 Serve hot or at room temperature topped with some sliced green onions, the remaining orange zest, and sesame seeds. Try this with a side of rice (page 179), garlic glazed bok choy (page 74), or smashed cucumber salad (page 53).

It's weird how mayonnaise became the default dressing for pasta salads. Like, did they try anything else? Pesto is straight-up delicious on its own, but in this recipe it really highlights the flavors of the summer ingredients. All we're saying is, if you had a spoonful of basil and a spoonful of mayonnaise in a blind taste test? Pesto's winning. Every fucking time. Now apply that logic to pasta salad.

BASIL PESTO SUMMER PASTA SALAD WITH SUNFLOWER SEEDS

1 Cook the pasta according to the package directions. We don't know what the fuck you're buying, so just trust the box. Before you drain the pasta, save 1 cup of that pasta water and set aside.

2 While the pasta is cooking, make the pesto.

3 When everything is ready, drain the pasta and put it in a large bowl with the corn, tomatoes, and cucumber. Add the pesto and toss to combine. If the pesto is too thick to coat the pasta, add a couple tablespoons of that pasta water to the bowl and thin that shit out. Taste and add salt, pepper, or some lemon juice if you think anything is missing.

4 Top with the sunflower seeds and serve at room temperature or you can let that shit chill in the fridge. Whatever you're feeling.

COOK TIME 25 MIN

>> **Makes enough for 4 to 6 people**

16 ounces uncooked pasta (we like bow ties or shells, but do whatever you like)

1 cup Basic Herb Pesto (page 184)

Kernels cut off of 2 ears of corn

2 cups sliced cherry or grape tomatoes

½ English cucumber or 2 Persian cucumbers, chopped

Salt and black pepper

Lemon juice (optional)

½ cup roasted sunflower seeds, salted or unsalted, whatever you got

If you want to make it a motherfucking meal, add some kind of additional protein like shelled edamame or chickpeas or our All-Seasons Tempeh Crumble (page 203).

COOK TIME 50 MIN

» **Makes about 6 sammies, depending on the size of the shrooms**

SHROOMS

1½ cups all-purpose or white rice flour

½ cup cornstarch

2 teaspoons Cajun or all-purpose seasoning blend

½ teaspoon baking powder

Salt

1 cup nondairy milk

1 teaspoon apple cider vinegar

1 tablespoon hot sauce, such as Crystal's

3 bundles maitake mushrooms, cut into 6 sandwich-size pieces

Peanut oil, for frying

SPICE MIX

2 tablespoons cayenne pepper

1 tablespoon brown sugar

1 teaspoon garlic powder

1 teaspoon smoked paprika

½ teaspoon ground ginger

1 teaspoon ground white pepper*

Remember when we collectively lost our minds over some basic-ass hot chicken sandwiches? Well we can't just let that go and not improve on it. This has all the heat and crunch of the original with none of the chicken. The flavor is loud as fuck and it's hard to eat just one. Go ahead and double the batch, just be prepared if cars start pulling up like a drive-thru.

NASHVILLE HOT SHROOM SAMMIE

1 For the shrooms: This is a dredge-and-fry kinda recipe, so we got to set shit up before we actually get cookin'. In a shallow bowl, whisk together the flour, cornstarch, Cajun seasoning, baking powder, and a pinch of salt. Then do the same shit with the milk, vinegar, hot sauce, and a pinch of salt in another shallow bowl.

2 Now, gently rinse off your mushroom slices and get to dredging. Dredge the mushrooms in the dry mixture first, then dunk in the milk mixture, then back into the dry. Keep one hand for the dry shit and the other for the wet, otherwise your hands will look like paste-covered claws that you can do nothing with. Transfer the dredged shrooms to a plate to hang out while you do the rest.

3 Pour 1 inch of peanut oil into a large, deep skillet over medium-high heat. When the oil is hot, CAREFULLY add the breaded mushrooms. Do three at a time. If you overcrowd the pan everything will be shitty, so do multiple batches. Fry until they are nice and golden brown all over, 3 to 4 minutes per side.

4 While the mushrooms are frying, get the spice mix ready: In a heatproof bowl, whisk together all the ingredients.

(continued)

THIS HEAT IS WORTH THE HYPE

SAMMIES

Shredded iceberg lettuce or cabbage

Nondairy mayonnaise

Salt

Hamburger buns or sandwich bread

Refrigerator Dill Pickles (page 196)

Sliced tomatoes

5 When you're done frying all the mushrooms, add about ½ cup hot frying oil to the bowl with the spices and whisk until smooth. BE CAREFUL 'CAUSE THAT SHIT IS HOT. Dunk the fried mushrooms in the spiced oil and then put them on a cooling rack so the extra sauce can drip off. If this sauce gets too thick at any point while you're dunking the mushrooms, just thin out with a little more hot oil.

6 Now make the fucking sammies: Toss the lettuce with a little mayo and a pinch of salt. Slather a bottom bun or piece of bread with mayo, then layer with pickles. Top with the shrooms, then lettuce and tomatoes. You know how to build a sandwich. Eat this shit right away.

* If you can't find this shit or don't wanna look, leave it out.

Skeptical about mushrooms? You've just been preparing them wrong. Learn all about them on page 241 and how they'll help you level up like Mario. Still wanna make this recipe but without all the fungi? Chop a head of cauliflower up into wings-sized bites and just use that instead. Now you got some finger-lickin' to do.

This is basically a fancy pizza using a classic overlooked veggie. Half y'all reading this couldn't even identify fennel right now, so this dish is an absolute food flex. Only we will know exactly how easy it is to make. Learn more about fennel on page 223 so you can actually find that shit in the store.

CARAMELIZED FENNEL TARTS

COOK TIME
60 MIN

>> **Makes 2 tarts with about 6 pieces each; enough for 6 to 8 as an appetizer, 2 to 4 as a main course**

2 tablespoons olive oil

2 medium bulbs fennel, thinly sliced, some fronds put aside to use later

½ white or red onion, thinly sliced

Salt

2 teaspoons fresh thyme, chopped

½ teaspoon grated lemon zest

¼ teaspoon black pepper

1 cup Cashew Cheese Sauce (page 213)

2 sheets frozen puff pastry,* thawed but still cold

* This is in the freezer section of the grocery store near the pie crusts. There are recipes out there on how to make this shit from scratch if you're into it, but that's a flex even we're too lazy for.

1 Heat the olive oil in a medium sauté pan over medium-high heat. Add the fennel, onion, and a pinch of salt. Sauté until they start to soften up just a little, 3 to 4 minutes. Reduce the heat to medium-low and cook, stirring occasionally, until the vegetables are caramelized into a nice, even brown color and have started smelling nice and sweet, 15 to 20 minutes. Fold in the thyme, lemon zest, and pepper and remove from the heat.

2 Crank the oven to 400°F. Grab a baking sheet and line it with parchment paper.

3 Put the 2 sheets puff pastry on the baking sheet and get ready. Spread ½ cup of the cashew cheese sauce over each piece of puff pastry, leaving a ¼-inch border around the pastry. You know, like a fucking pizza. This is just a fancy pizza. You're in on the secret.

4 Place half of the fennel-onion mixture down on top of the cheese sauce, and gently press down so the fennel and onions are not just floating on top. Throw this all in the oven and bake until the puff pastry turns golden brown around the edges, 15 to 20 minutes.

5 Let this cool for a couple minutes before serving.

MOST ROOTY OR LEAFY VEGGIES SCRAPS WILL REGENERATE IN A COUPLE INCHES OF WATER.

1 Beet
2 Green Onion
3 Flowering Broccoli
4 Lettuces
5 Russet Potato
6 Garlic
7 Leek
8 Spinach
9 Herbs
10 Lettuce
11 Spring Onions
12 Celery
13 Worm
14 Red Onion

PLUS YOU CAN AVOID UNCOMFORTABLE SMALL TALK WITH STRANGERS BY TELLING THEM YOU NEED TO CHANGE THE WATER IN YOUR ZOMBIE GARDEN.

SLURPING ISN'T BAD MANNERS
IT'S JUST GOOD FOOD

We love this dish so fucking much that it was almost on the cover of this book. But the publisher thought it looked like worms, so here we are. Slurp up motherfuckers, it's worm-free.

TERIYAKI JACKFRUIT WITH CURRY UDON NOODLES

COOK TIME 50 MIN

»» Makes enough for 4 people

1 First we're gonna make the curry noodles: Cook them according to the package directions and drain.

2 While the noodles are draining, use that same pot to make the sauce. Set it over medium-high heat and add the oil. Throw in the onion and bell pepper and cook until they both soften up a little, about 3 minutes. Add the garlic and curry powder and sauté for another 30 seconds, until everything is covered in the powder. Add the tamari and milk and remove the curry sauce from the heat. We gotta multitask here, so we're coming back to this shit in a sec.

3 Now we mix up the teriyaki sauce: Grab a small glass and mix together the cornstarch, vinegar, maple syrup, tamari, and sesame oil, making sure there are no clumps. Stir in the garlic and set that shit aside.

4 Cook the jackfruit: In a skillet, heat the oil over medium heat. Add the jackfruit, shallot, and ginger and stir it all around, breaking up the jackfruit more with whatever you're stirring with. Let this cook for 5 to 7 minutes so that the shallot and jackfruit start to get a little brown in some spots. Stir that teriyaki sauce we made a few minutes ago and pour it over the jackfruit. We swear you're almost fucking done. Cook, stirring frequently, to coat the jackfruit as the sauce thickens up, 1 to 2 minutes. When the sauce looks nice and thick and all the jackfruit is coated, remove from the heat.

CURRY NOODLES

16 ounces udon or rice noodles (the fattest you can find), cooked according to the package directions

1 tablespoon neutral oil, such as safflower

½ red onion, sliced

1 red bell pepper, sliced

2 garlic cloves, minced

2 tablespoons no-salt curry powder

1 tablespoon tamari or soy sauce

½ cup nondairy milk

TERIYAKI JACKFRUIT

1 teaspoon cornstarch

¼ cup rice vinegar

¼ cup pure maple syrup

¼ cup tamari or soy sauce

1 tablespoon toasted sesame oil

1 large clove garlic, minced

1 tablespoon neutral oil, such as safflower

(continued)

1 can (20 ounces) jackfruit, drained and rinsed, and broken apart with your hands*

1 shallot, diced

2 tablespoons minced fresh ginger

TO FINISH

4 cups chopped greens, such as spinach or baby bok choy

1 tablespoon fresh lime juice or Fresh Chile Vinegar (page 211)

¼ cup chopped fresh cilantro

¼ cup chopped green onions

5 Now to finish: Turn back to the noodles. Warm the pot of curry sauce back up to a simmer, then add the drained noodles and the chopped greens. Cook for a minute or two just so that the noodles can absorb all the sauce and the greens can wilt down, 1 to 2 minutes. Remove from the heat, add the lime juice, and taste. Add more soy, curry powder, or whateverthefuck you think it needs. Done.

6 To serve, put a whole mess of noodles at the bottom of a bowl, sprinkle with the cilantro and green onions, and add some jackfruit to the middle of the bowl. This will make you forget about the shitty take-out mess you usually eat.

Scared of jackfruit? Educate thyself on page 239.

 Too much at one time? Make the noodles ahead of time and warm them up when the jackfruit is ready to make dinner go faster.

You start this rice out on the stovetop and then bake it uncovered to finish it off. It doesn't seem like this shit should make some of the best rice you've ever had, but we swear that it does. The fresh mint brings all the summer flavors together, but most people won't be able to figure out what the hell it is that makes this taste so good. We won't tell if you don't.

BAKED EGGPLANT RICE

1 Crank the oven to 400°F.

2 Warm up your largest ovenproof skillet over medium-high heat and add 2 tablespoons of the oil. Throw in the eggplant and stir until it's all coated in oil. Add a pinch of salt and sauté until the eggplant starts to soften, about 5 minutes. You'll know. Add the onion and sauté until the onion starts to look translucent, another 3 minutes. Add the tomatoes with all their juices and the garlic and cook for an additional minute, just so all the flavors start mixing.

3 Add ½ teaspoon salt, the pepper, oregano, parsley, mint, and rice and stir until everything is all mixed together. Stir in the veggie broth, vinegar, and drizzle with the remaining 1 tablespoon oil. This will probably look full as hell, but don't worry. Remove from the heat 'cause it's time to get baked.

4 Place in the oven carefully since it is all kinds of full, and bake until all the liquid has been absorbed and the rice is tender, 25 to 30 minutes. Remove from the oven, fluff the rice with a fork, and add the lemon juice. Fluff again and then taste and add whateverthefuck you think it needs. Top with more fresh mint and parsley and serve right away in the skillet or in another bowl if you love doing dishes. (Got leftovers and wanna stuff some peppers? Head to page 142.)

COOK TIME 45 MIN

» **Makes enough for 4 to 6 people**

3 tablespoons olive oil

1 large eggplant,* chopped (about 6 cups)

½ teaspoon salt, plus more as needed

1 large yellow onion, chopped (about 3 cups)

4 fist-sized tomatoes, chopped (about 2½ cups)

6 garlic cloves, minced

¼ teaspoon black pepper

2 teaspoons dried oregano

¼ cup minced fresh parsley

2 tablespoons minced fresh mint

1½ cups long-grain rice

3 cups vegetable broth

2 tablespoons red wine vinegar

Juice of 1 lemon

Learn more about the delicious weirdness of eggplant on page 233.

>> **Makes enough for 4 people**

3 tablespoons neutral oil, such as safflower

1 large onion, chopped

2 cans (20 ounces each) jackfruit,* drained and rinsed, and kinda broken apart with your hands so it looks like shredded pork

4 garlic cloves, minced

2 cups cola (sweetened with cane sugar)

1 cup vegetable broth

2 tablespoons pomegranate molasses

2 tablespoons Bragg Liquid Aminos**

2 teaspoons smoked paprika

2 teaspoons liquid smoke**

½ cup pomegranate seeds***

¼ cup minced fresh parsley

Learn more about jackfruit on page 239.

** WTF? See page 180.

*** Don't know shit about pomegranates? Turn to page 244.

This recipe is so good it doesn't need a header. Just read the name and look at the fucking photo on page 90.

POMEGRANATE COLA JACKFRUIT

1 In a large ovenproof skillet, heat 1 tablespoon of the oil over medium heat. Add the onion and sauté until it starts to brown, 5 to 8 minutes. Add the jackfruit and garlic and stir it to break up the jackfruit more. Cook this until the jackfruit is getting some color on it, about 5 minutes.

2 While that is cooking, in a large glass, mix together the cola, broth, pomegranate molasses, Bragg's, smoked paprika, and liquid smoke. When the jackfruit looks good, pour this mixture over it, stir, and let that fucker simmer, uncovered, over medium-low heat for about 30 minutes or until two-thirds of the liquid has evaporated.

3 While that is simmering, crank the oven to 450°F.

4 Remove the jackfruit from the heat and stir in the remaining 2 tablespoons oil. Stick this shit in the oven and let it roast until the top layer of jackfruit starts to look dry and some corners are starting to look a little burnt, 15 to 20 minutes.

5 Stir and taste, then add more of whatever you like. Serve warm topped with pomegranate seeds and parsley.

 Pomegranate molasses is like a fruitier, way more fucking interesting molasses and should be near the liquid sweeteners or falafel mix in your grocery store. Can't find it? Look on the fucking Internet or leave it out for an okay but not nearly as delicious meal.

HOW TO BAKE TOFU

Everybody is scared of tofu. Yeah, this shit can be bland and mushy, but that is because people don't know how to cook it right and it's annoying as hell. It isn't hard, most fuckers are just lazy about it. We got shit all figured out, though. Throw tofu in a flavorful marinade and then bake it at high heat and it turns into something worth eating . . . not just a health food dare. Try it out and see how much better you can be at this tofuckery than everybody else.

Grab some extra-firm tofu, drain it, wrap it in some paper towels or a clean tea towel, put it between two plates, and throw some weight on top. We like some cans. The weight presses out all the water the tofu is packed in and makes room for flavor. Let this press for about 30 minutes to 1 hour. Go take a nap or something.

Next, mix together your marinade in a shallow, rimmed dish like a pie pan, something where all the tofu can marinate in one layer.

Cut the tofu widthwise into planks no thicker than ¼ inch. You should get about 12 pieces per brick of tofu. Throw the planks in the marinade, make sure all the pieces are covered, and let that sit in the fridge for at least 2 hours and up to 8. Stir it around every now and then if you remember.

When you're ready, preheat the oven to 450°F. Grease a sheet pan.

Take the tofu out of the marinade (but keep the marinade). Arrange the tofu on the pan and bake for 15 minutes. Flip the tofu over, spoon some marinade on top of each piece, and bake for 10 more minutes. Flip and sauce again and bake for a final 5 minutes. The edges should start looking a little burnt. That's the fucking way to do it, so calm down.

Pull it out of the oven and let it sit for a couple minutes to firm up and cool down and then cut it into the shapes you need. Baked marinated tofu is great folded into salads and pastas where you need some extra protein but regular beans would seem fucked up.

On the following two pages, we've got a couple of our favorite marinades for tofu. You got this shit.

» Makes enough for 2 to 4 people

1 block (14 ounces) extra-firm tofu

½ cup roughly chopped shallots

¼ cup roughly chopped lemongrass* (from the white inner part of 2 stalks)

1-inch piece fresh ginger, roughly chopped

2 garlic cloves, minced

3 tablespoons brown sugar

1 tablespoon chili-garlic paste

¼ cup soy sauce

¼ cup fresh lime juice (2 to 3 limes)

2 tablespoons Maggi Seasoning**

2 tablespoons rice vinegar

1 tablespoon neutral oil, such as safflower

Scared of lemongrass? Read up on page 240 and cook with some fucking confidence.

*** WTF? See page 136.*

You can never have too many tofu recipes in your life. And this one is bright, savory, and the perfect side to our Bok Choy with Garlic (page 74) and Shredded Daikon Salad (page 54). Add some rice and you got a plate of food that your mom would be proud of.

LEMONGRASS BAKED TOFU

1 Drain the tofu and wrap it in several layers of paper towels or a tea towel. Place it on a plate and put another plate on top of it. Place 1 or 2 large soup cans on the top plate and press the tofu for at least 30 minutes and up to 2 hours. It's not gonna get flat or any shit like that. We're just getting that flavorless liquid out.

2 While the tofu is being pressed, in a shallow dish (like a loaf pan or pie plate), mix together all the remaining ingredients to make the marinade. Check for flavor and adjust the seasoning as necessary. Set aside.

3 When the tofu is ready to go, lay it flat on a cutting board. Cut ⅛- to ¼-inch-thick slices off the tofu from the short end. You should end up with 10 to 12 pieces if you know how to measure shit. Place them in the marinade and let them sit for at least 30 minutes or up to 1½ hours, flipping the tofu over halfway through.

4 When you're ready to bake, crank the oven to 400°F. Heavily grease a large sheet pan.

5 Place the marinated tofu slices on the sheet pan a couple of inches apart. Reserve the remaining marinade. Bake for 15 minutes. Flip the tofu slices and bake for another 10 minutes. Flip the tofu one more time if needed to even out the color but only if you care about that shit.

6 Spoon over some of the remaining marinade and bake until the tofu looks somewhat blackened on both sides and slightly crispy, another 5 to 10 minutes. Trust the process.

7 Take the tofu out of the oven and spoon over a little more marinade. The tofu will firm up slightly as it cools on the pan and absorbs the rest of the marinade. Let it cool for about 5 minutes.

8 Cut into smaller pieces if you prefer and serve warm, at room temp, or cold. It's good no matter what.

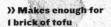
》Makes enough for 1 brick of tofu

¼ cup soy sauce or tamari

¼ cup rice vinegar

2 tablespoons fresh lime juice

2 tablespoons brown sugar

1 tablespoon minced fresh ginger

2 teaspoons toasted sesame oil

2 teaspoons Sriracha or similar hot sauce

½ teaspoon ground turmeric or your favorite no-salt curry powder

GINGER-TURMERIC TOFU MARINADE

Mix all the ingredients together in a rimmed dish and use it to marinate 1 brick of tofu as directed on the opposite page.

>> **Makes about 30 tamales**

CHIPOTLE SAUCE

3 canned chipotle peppers in adobo sauce*

¼ cup vegetable broth

¼ cup fresh lime juice (2 to 3 limes)

2 tablespoons oil

½ white onion, roughly chopped

2 garlic cloves, peeled

½ teaspoon salt

½ teaspoon ground cumin

¼ teaspoon dried oregano

FILLING

1 small spaghetti squash (about 1½ pounds)

1 small pumpkin or kabocha squash (about 2 pounds)**

½ white onion, minced

1 tablespoon pure maple syrup

* You'll find these spicy motherfuckers in a small can near the jarred salsa at the store.

** Learn all about pumpkins and gourd life on page 247.

Yes, making tamales takes a while, but yes, it's always fucking worth it. This recipe makes a ton of tamales and they freeze and reheat perfectly so you can eat these corn-husk-wrapped babies whenever you get a craving.

CHIPOTLE PUMPKIN TAMALES

1 Crank the oven to 400°F. Oil a large baking sheet.

2 While the oven is preheating, make the chipotle sauce: Throw the chipotles in adobo, broth, lime juice, oil, onion, garlic, salt, cumin, and oregano in a food processor or blender and let that fucker run until everything is relatively smooth looking. Set it aside.

3 Make the filling: Cut the spaghetti squash and pumpkin in half and scoop out the seeds and stringy stuff. Place them cut-side down on the baking sheet and roast them until you can push a fork through their flesh with no resistance, 30 to 40 minutes. A fucking brutal sentence, but that's how it goes.

4 When the pumpkin and spaghetti squash are cool enough to handle, scoop the pumpkin flesh into a bowl and smash it up kinda like mashed potatoes. You want about 1½ cups. Yes, you could use a can of pumpkin for this, but it tastes better and is less mushy when you do this yourself. Now, using a fork, scrape out the insides of the spaghetti squash so you get those long strands that give the squash its name. Some chunks are cool, you're not making baby food. Dump this in with the pumpkin. Now fold in the reserved chipotle sauce, the onion, and maple syrup and set that shit aside.

5 Now finally we start with the masa dough: You can do all the other steps ahead of time, but you don't wanna make your masa until you're ready to make the tamales. Got it? You're gonna need a stand mixer or hand mixer for this shit. In a large bowl or your stand mixer, add the shortening and whip it until it looks fluffy, kinda like frosting. In a medium bowl, whisk together the masa harina, baking powder, salt, and spices. Add one-quarter of the masa mixture at a time to the shortening, beating between additions until everything is all mixed in. It will start looking all sandy, which is good. When you've added all the masa, pour in the vegetable broth while continuing to beat it until all the liquid is absorbed and the dough starts to look all fluffy again, about 5 minutes. There shouldn't be any dry spots and you should be able to press your whole hand into the dough and it should come out clean. Done and done.

6 Now we make our tamales. Place a soaked corn husk on a cutting board with the wide end facing away from you and the tapered end closer to you. For each tamale, plop about 3 tablespoons of dough in the center of the corn husk about ½ inch from the wide end, which we're calling the top from here on out. Pat the dough into an oblong shape about ¼ inch thick, leaving a 1½-inch border of uncovered husk on either side of the dough. Scoop up 2 tablespoons of filling and place it down the center of the masa rectangle you just made. Grab those uncovered edges of corn husk and bring them toward each other to lift the dough toward the center, and press the dough to now surround the filling. Gently fold those edges of corn husk so that they overlap one another to cover the dough and wrap them around the whole tamale. If you still have some extra husk, no big deal. Fold the long tapered end up to form a squat little rectangular package. Use a thin strip of corn husk to tie the tamale together in the middle, which also keeps the tapered end of the corn husk in place. The top of the tamale stays open so you can cheat and see when these guys are cooked all the way. You're welcome. Repeat with remaining dough, filling, and husks. When you're almost done assembling tamales, get the steaming pot ready.

7 You know that big metal steamer insert that came with your big-ass pasta pot and that you've never used? Now is the time. Fill that large pot with only enough water so that it does not touch the steamer basket, 3 to 4 inches, depending on your pot and basket, obvs. Cover and bring to a boil.

MASA DOUGH

1¼ cups vegetable shortening

3¾ cups masa harina**

2 teaspoons baking powder

1 tablespoon salt

1 tablespoon smoked paprika

2 teaspoons garlic powder

2 teaspoons onion powder

2½ cups vegetable broth

About 40 dried corn husks,*** soaked in water for at least 15 minutes

** No clue what this is? See page 181.

*** These should be near the dried chiles at your local market.

(continued)

8 Grab that metal steamer insert and line it with a couple of the extra corn husks to help keep the tamales from getting wet while they steam. Stand the assembled tamales with the open ends facing up in the lined steamer insert, but don't pack them in too tight, leave a little bit of room to allow the tamales to expand during steaming. You don't need a ton of room, just don't smush them all in there and ruin all your hard work. Place the tamale-filled steamer over the steaming pot of water and put on the lid.

9 Steam the tamales until the dough starts to peel away from the husk, 45 to 55 minutes. Leaving that one end open lets you check on them without opening a fuck-ton of them. You can just kinda glance. Check the pot occasionally to make sure that not all of the water has evaporated, adding more hot, not cold, water if you need to. When they look down to you, pull one tamale out and peel back that husk. In a fully cooked tamale, the masa will be tender but solid, not mushy or wet looking, and the husk will peel away easily. Remove the entire basket with the lid from the pot and let stand for 8 minutes to cool before serving.

10 Serve this warm, right away, with your favorite salsa. Let people peel off the husks themselves, don't do this ahead of time. If you're freezing some of these, let them cool to room temp and place them in a plastic bag or container and stick them in the freezer like a present to future you.

This might sound weird as fuck but it's the perfect summer dish and makes so much sense in your mouth. The first time we made this we served it to a friend who proudly stated it was "the best damn spaghetti I've ever had." And while this shit isn't spaghetti, his point stands. It's damn good.

GRILLED NECTARINE SOBA NOODLES

1 Cook the noodles according to the package directions because they know better than you.

2 While that's going, scrape the skin off the ginger with a spoon, then chop it up into tiny-ass pieces so that you end up with about 3 tablespoons. In a small glass, combine the ginger, water, soy sauce, vinegar, sesame oil, and 2 tablespoons of the lemon juice and mix that shit up.

3 When the noodles are done cooking, drain 'em and rinse with cold water.

4 Cut the nectarines into slices no bigger than 1 inch. (You can leave the skin on because EVERYBODY COULD USE MORE FIBER.) In a large bowl, mix together the remaining 1 tablespoon lemon juice, the neutral oil, 5-spice powder, and salt. Throw the sliced nectarines in there and make sure they get covered in that spice blend shit.

5 Bring your grill to a medium-high heat and spray the grates with a lil oil so the nectarines don't stick. Place the nectarines on there for 45 seconds or so on each side. You don't need to cook them, you just want some char marks on there because that's pro. Grilling them also caramelizes the natural sugars in those making them slightly sweeter.

6 Toss the noodles with the sauce you already made and add the watercress. Pile the grilled nectarines on top and serve.

COOK TIME
35 MIN

》 **Makes enough for 4 to 6**

12 ounces soba or other uncooked thin noodles

1-inch piece fresh ginger

¼ cup water

¼ cup soy sauce or tamari

3 tablespoons rice vinegar

2 tablespoons toasted sesame oil

3 tablespoons fresh lemon juice

2 fist-size nectarines, ripe but not super soft

1 tablespoon neutral oil, such as grapeseed

1 tablespoon fresh lemon juice

2 teaspoons Chinese 5-spice powder*

Pinch of salt

½ to ¾ cup chopped watercress**

* Most grocery stores carry this shit. If you can't find it, use a bit of cinnamon and pepper.

** Cilantro, arugula, spinach, or even green onions would work too.

COOK TIME 85 MIN

>> **Makes enough for 4 people**

1 tablespoon neutral high-heat oil, like safflower

4 big bundles of maitake or oyster mushrooms*

MARINADE

2 tablespoons neutral high-heat oil, like safflower

½ cup lime juice, from about 4 limes

½ cup chopped fresh cilantro

¼ cup orange juice

6 garlic cloves, minced

2 tablespoons Bragg Liquid Aminos**

1 or 2 jalapeños, minced

1 tablespoon chili powder

2 teaspoons ground cumin

Spray oil, like safflower

As most of y'all know by now, Matt was born and raised in Texas. Cooking carne asada is as much a part of life as boots and belt buckles. What y'all probably don't know is Matt fucking HATES mushrooms. Portobello burgers are a crime against food. Seriously, that shit tastes like an old sponge soaked in sweat. But after a shitload of experimenting, looking at beakers and murmuring "science" every once in a while, we successfully remedied Matt's disdain for mushrooms by indulging his love for asada. This recipe delivers the taste and texture we all crave from asada but, ya know, without the bovine butt.

SHROOM ASADA

1 First, heat up a skillet over medium-high heat and pour in the oil. Throw in the mushrooms and put something heavy on top of them so they flatten while they sear. A smaller pan or even a brick wrapped in foil would work. We want all that water in the mushrooms to get the fuck out so we can put some flavor in there. Kinda like how we tell y'all to cook tofu. Same idea. After about 3 or 4 minutes, they should look seared and brown in some places plus, ya know, flattened. Flip and repeat. When they're done, put the mushrooms in a rimmed baking dish or large tray to cool while you mix up the marinade.

2 Throw all the marinade ingredients in a large blender and pulse until everything's combined. Large chunks are okay. Pour that over the seared mushrooms and let 'em sit at least an hour and up to 3 hours in the fridge.

3 When it's time to get cooking, you've got two choices: grill or pan-sear. Grilling is gonna you the best char and texture, but if you can't make that shit work then pan-searing is fine too.

4 To grill, warm the grill pan or BBQ to a medium-high heat and oil the grill grate. Pull the mushrooms out of the marinade and spray them lightly with some oil. Place them on the hot grill top and let them roast for 3 to 5 minutes on each side. You already cooked 'em earlier, remember, so you're really just looking for some char and those sexy grill marks. Take the shrooms off when they look good enough for your personal asada aesthetic.

5 To sear, follow the same process using a medium-high heat. Just do NOT grab a nonstick pan. You want something like cast-iron so you can get some burn on those bad boys. When the mushrooms are done you can serve them up whole or slice them and kinda fan 'em out over a serving plate with some leftover marinade drizzled on top. Can't do that shit with red meat because the marinade would be tainted as hell.

* Learn more about mushrooms on page 241.

** WTF? See page 180.

The asada is best when served with a side of warm tortillas, sliced radishes, jalapenos, avocado, and pico de gallo or our Roasted Corn Salsa (page 79). Chop up anything left over and toss them over some nachos the next day.

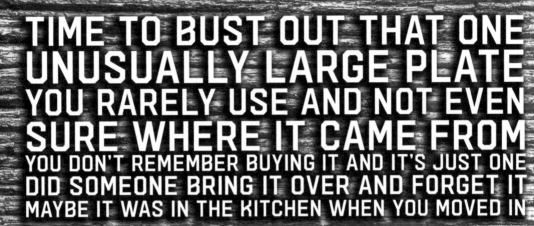
TIME TO BUST OUT THAT ONE
UNUSUALLY LARGE PLATE
YOU RARELY USE AND NOT EVEN
SURE WHERE IT CAME FROM
YOU DON'T REMEMBER BUYING IT AND IT'S JUST ONE
DID SOMEONE BRING IT OVER AND FORGET IT
MAYBE IT WAS IN THE KITCHEN WHEN YOU MOVED IN

>> **Makes about 24 pupusas**

PUPUSA FILLING

2 teaspoons olive or safflower oil

1 small white onion, diced

1 can (20 ounces) jackfruit*

2 tablespoons soy sauce or Bragg Liquid Aminos**

1 teaspoon smoked paprika

1 teaspoon ground cumin

½ teaspoon dried oregano

3 garlic cloves, minced

1 medium tomato, diced

1½ cups cooked black beans, pinto, or refried beans or 1 can (15 ounces), drained and rinsed

PUPUSA DOUGH

4 cups masa harina**

2 teaspoons salt

2 tablespoons olive or safflower oil

2¾ cups water

Safflower oil

FOR SERVING

Curtido (page 78)

Your favorite hot sauce

We have a pupuseria near our office that we've been eating at for years. We were tired of having to drive down there whenever we got a craving so we made our own. Now we don't even hafta search for parking.

JACKFRUIT PUPUSAS

1 Make the filling: In a large skillet, heat the oil over medium-high heat. Add the onion and sauté until it starts to brown, 7 to 10 minutes. Add the garlic, prepped jackfruit, soy sauce, and spices and cook until parts of the jackfruit look golden brown, about 8 minutes.

2 Transfer half the jackfruit to a food processor and add the tomato and beans. Pulse until a thick paste forms. Fold that paste in with the stuff left in the pan. It's called texture, motherfuckers. Gotta keep it interesting.

3 While the filling cools, make the pupusa dough: In a large bowl, whisk together the masa harina and salt, then add the oil and water. Use your hands to mix until the dough comes together and kinda feels like Play-Doh. You don't want it super wet and sticky. It just needs to hold its shape and not have any dry spots. Easy.

4 OK, now we're gonna make the damn things. You're aiming for a pancake shape with the filling inside in a uniform layer. Don't stress if your first batch of pupusas look thicker than the photo. Getting your technique right takes time, practice, and finesse. Here we go.

5 Fill a small bowl with water and a bit of oil and set it near you. You'll want to wet your fingers as you work to keep the dough from sticking to your hands. Gotta think ahead. Now, take a chunk of dough the size of a golf ball and flatten into an even, round disk. Put 1 to 2 tablespoons of the jackfruit mix in

(continued)

THE ORIGINAL HOT POCKET

the middle of the dough round. Then fold the dough disk over the filling until it's completely sealed. Then pat out the ball between your hands until flat and shape the edges back into a disk. If the pupusa cracks, patch it with a bit of dough and a little oil and water. Nobody will fucking know. Put your finished pupusas on a large plate or baking sheet and keep up the assembly line until you're all out of dough or filling. Ideally this will happen at the same time, but shit happens.

6 When you're ready to cook them up, heat a large skillet or griddle over medium heat. Add 1 tablespoon safflower oil in the pan, warm that up, then place 2 or 3 pupusas in the pan and cook until the bottoms are golden brown, 2 to 4 minutes. Flip and cook on the other side until golden brown and warmed through, 2 to 4 minutes more. Are the pupusas sticking to your shitty pan? Try brushing the oil on the pupusas rather than putting it in the pan. Repeat with the remaining pupusas until everything is cooked and looking delicious.

7 Serve with the curtido and hot sauce. These freeze like a fucking dream.

* Don't know what the fuck jackfruit is? We got you. See page 239.

** WTF? See page 180.

*** No clue what this is? Go to page 181.

Pupusas are the perfect food to stock in the freezer. Wrap 2 at a time with a little plastic wrap and stick 'em in the freezer to grab whenever you're feeling lazy but still want a home-cooked meal. They reheat fine in the microwave, but we like to wrap them in foil and throw them in the oven at 350°F for 15 minutes. And obviously you gotta have jar of curtido (page 78) on standby in your fridge.

Skip the takeout and take yourself on a goddamn flavor flight to parts unknown. This tofu is crispy, sweet, and easy as hell to make. It is so good you'll def forget you're eating a cake made of beans. Check out the photo on page 94 if you're still not sold.

>> **Makes enough for 4 people**

STICKY TOFU WITH SWEET SESAME SAUCE

1 Wrap the tofu in a clean towel or some paper towels and set something heavy like a pan on top to wick away any moisture. Let it get squashed there for about 10 minutes.

2 While the tofu is pressing, in a small glass, combine the tamari, Maggi, mirin, and chili-garlic paste to make a marinade.

3 When the tofu has released a lot of its water or when 10 minutes has passed, chop it up into cubes about the size of a quarter, place 'em in a bowl, and drown those bitches with the marinade. Let that sit, mixing them around occasionally, for at least 20 minutes and up to 2 hours.

4 When you're ready to get this shit goin', make the sesame sauce: Grab a small glass and mix the sesame oil, garlic, vinegar, maple syrup, tamari, and cornstarch, making sure there's no clumps. Set that aside. That's that sauce in the photo that made you wanna cook this shit in the first place.

5 To finish, place the white rice flour in a wide bowl and drain the marinating tofu. Throw the tofu in the rice flour and toss to coat all the lil tofu pieces in the flour.

6 Heat a large skillet over medium heat with the oil. Use a slotted spoon to get the coated tofu out the extra flour and into the hot pan. Toss the tofu around in the pan until all the

TOFU

12 ounces extra-firm tofu

2 tablespoons tamari or soy sauce

2 tablespoons Maggi Seasoning*

2 tablespoons mirin or apple juice

1 teaspoon chili-garlic paste or Sriracha

SWEET SESAME SAUCE

1 tablespoon toasted sesame oil

1 large clove garlic, minced

¼ cup rice vinegar

¼ cup pure maple syrup

¼ cup tamari or soy sauce

2 tablespoons cornstarch

WTF? See page 180.

(continued)

½ cup white rice flour or cornstarch

2 tablespoons neutral oil, such as peanut or safflower

1 shallot, diced

2 tablespoons minced fresh ginger

Optional garnishes: Chopped cilantro, chopped green onions, or sesame seeds

pieces have a coating of oil. Cook the pieces on as many sides as possible for at least 1 minute or till light golden brown. When most of the tofu looks good, toss in the shallot and ginger and cook for about 30 seconds. Stir the teriyaki sauce around to make sure everything is incorporated, then pour it over the tofu in the hot pan.

7 You're almost done, so don't get lost in the sauce now. Cook, stirring frequently, to coat the tofu as the sauce thickens up, 1 to 2 minutes. When the sauce looks nice and thick and all the tofu is coated, remove from the heat.

8 Serve just like this or top it with some cilantro, green onions, or sesame seeds to really flex on the terrible takeout you usually settle for.

The trick to a good avocado-coconut curry is to get an avocado that is a day or two out from being soft. You don't want it rock hard and you don't want that shit mushy either. That's legit the hardest part of the recipe: buying the right damn avocado. Turn to page 220 to read all about how to pick one out and why you should eat them all the damn time.

COCONUT GREEN CURRY WITH AVOCADO

>> **Makes enough for 4 to 6 people**

1 In a large skillet or wok, heat the oil over medium-high heat. Add the curry paste and ginger and cook, stirring, until it starts smelling good, about 30 seconds. Add the onion, bell pepper, carrot, sugar snap peas, bamboo shoots, and bok choy and cook until everything is starting to get a little softer, about 3 minutes. Yeah, this shit moves fast at the beginning. Add the coconut milk and veggie broth and bring to a simmer. Add the tofu, avocado, salt, and sugar. Cook at a slow simmer until the veggies are tender but not mushy, about 10 minutes. Add the lime juice and remove from the heat.

2 Serve warm over rice or just as is. Top with basil or cilantro and more lime juice.

* You can use store-bought, or we got a recipe for you on page 214.

** You can find these guys in a can near the coconut milk the grocery store. Coming up empty? Leaves these fuckers out.

*** Need some tofu help? See page 181.

1 tablespoon coconut or safflower oil

2 to 3 tablespoons green curry paste*

1 tablespoon chopped fresh ginger

¼ white onion, sliced

1 bell pepper, chopped into chunks

1 carrot, chopped into ¼-inch-thick rounds

1 cup sugar snap peas

½ cup bamboo shoots**

3 heads of baby bok choy, sliced

2 cans (15 ounces each) full-fat coconut milk

1 cup vegetable broth

15 ounces extra-firm tofu, chopped into nickel-sized bites***

1 avocado, cut into chunks

¼ teaspoon salt

1 tablespoon cane sugar

2 tablespoons fresh lime juice, plus extra for garnish

3 cups cooked jasmine rice or short-grain brown rice (page 179)

¼ cup torn basil or chopped cilantro, for garnish

TECHNICALLY A FRUIT PIE

Not gonna lie, this is just a classy-ass pizza. Tart just sounds much fancier when dishing it up. Tomatoes are abundant as fuck in the summer so, throw a motherfuckin' pizz . . . uhh, a motherfuckin' tart party.

SUMMER TOMATO TART

1 First, pick your pesto and make that shit.

2 When you're ready to tart it up, crank the oven to 400°F. Line a large baking sheet with some parchment paper.

3 Roll the puff pastry into squarish shapes. Put the puff pastry on the baking sheet and spread a couple spoonfuls of the pesto over the pastry leaving a ½-inch border around the edges. Like a fucking pizza, okay?

4 Sprinkle the basil over the pesto and then arrange the tomatoes in a single layer and press them a little into the pesto so they don't slide around. Sprinkle some salt and pepper on top and spread on the cashew cheese sauce (if you're using that shit). Now repeat with the other piece of puff pastry.

5 Bake until the pastry is golden brown and well, puffed, 15 to 20 minutes. Let it cool for 5 minutes before serving.

* Puff pastry should be near the frozen pie crusts in a grocery store.

** These can be whatever the fuck kind of large, ripe tomatoes you can find (but heirlooms always look the prettiest). Try to mix up the colors, though, because that really says "I KNOW HOW TO MAKE A FUCKING TART." Read up on tomatoes on page 247.

COOK TIME 30 MIN

» **Makes 2 square tarts**

½ recipe Sun-Dried Tomato Pesto (page 185) or Basic Herb Pesto (page 184)

2 sheets puff pastry*

½ cup chopped fresh basil

4 large tomatoes,** cut into ¼-inch-thick slices (like you were putting them on a burger)

Salt and black pepper

½ cup Cashew Cheese Sauce (optional; page 213)

» **Makes enough for 4 people**

6 saffron threads*

2 cups vegetable broth

1 pound uncooked long pasta, like spaghetti or fettuccine

35 zucchini blossoms, stems removed (about 5 ounces)

3 tablespoons olive oil

1 large onion, thinly sliced

Salt

2½ cups chopped zucchini or other soft summer squash** (about 2 medium)

½ pound cherry tomatoes, halved

6 garlic cloves, minced

1 teaspoon red pepper flakes

2 tablespoons fresh lemon juice

2 tablespoons finely chopped fresh flat-leaf parsley

This is your summer pasta recipe when you want to feel like you're having a fancy night out without having to cook for two days straight. Squash blossoms aren't in the markets for very long so if you see them, buy them immediately, and make this for dinner that night. Feast on some flowers.

ZUCCHINI BLOSSOM PASTA

1 In a bowl, add the saffron threads to the vegetable broth and let those bougie fuckers steep while you cook everything else.

2 Cook the pasta according to the damn package. Drain and set aside.

3 While that shit gets going, gently rinse and dry the zucchini blossoms. In a medium skillet, warm up 1 tablespoon of the oil and sauté the blossoms, gently turning them until they wilt, 1 to 2 minutes. Remove from the heat and place them on a plate for later.

4 Add the rest of the oil to the same pan and warm over medium heat. Add the onion with a pinch of salt and sauté until it starts to get a little golden, 5 to 7 minutes. Add the zucchini and tomatoes and cook until the tomatoes start to break down, another 5 minutes. Add ½ teaspoon salt, the garlic, and pepper flakes and stir to combine.

5 Take the saffron threads out of the broth. Add the lemon juice and saffron veggie broth to the pot, stir, and toss in the drained pasta. Reduce the heat and keep stirring until the pasta has absorbed most of the broth, then remove from the heat. Fold in the squash blossoms and sprinkle with parsley. Serve right away.

No saffron? Just leave that shit out.

** *Don't know your squashes? Go to page 246 to learn.*

SERVE UP SUMMER

» **Makes enough for 6 people**

6 large tomatoes or bell peppers*

2 tablespoons olive oil, plus more for drizzling

1 white or yellow onion, chopped

4 garlic cloves, minced

1 teaspoon dried oregano

1 teaspoon dried thyme

1 teaspoon red pepper flakes, or less, depending on if you can hang

½ teaspoon salt

¼ teaspoon black pepper

1 cup white or brown basmati rice, rinsed

1½ to 1¾ cups vegetable broth*

1½ cups cooked chickpeas, white beans, or cannellini beans or 1 can (15 ounces), drained and rinsed

2 tablespoons fresh lemon juice or red wine vinegar

¼ cup roughly chopped fresh parsley, plus more for garnish

¼ cup roughly chopped fresh mint, plus more for garnish

You can throw any kind of rice or grain-based dish into some bell peppers or tomatoes and it's an instant upgrade. But if you're starting from scratch, i.e., not using leftover, we're here to show you the ropes with this old family recipe we've been fucking with.

Using leftover rice? Add some beans or our All-Seasons Tempeh Crumble (page 203) and make that shit stretch further. This is also a great place to use the leftovers from our Baked Eggplant Rice (page 119) or Tomato Rice (page 85). Just fill and follow the baking instructions below.

TOULATOS-STYLE STUFFED TOMATOES OR BELL PEPPERS

1 Grease a medium baking dish with a lid (or you can cover it with foil).

2 Cut off the tops of the tomatoes or bell peppers and set the tops aside. YOU NEED THOSE FUCKERS LATER. If using tomatoes, hollow them out, and chop enough of the flesh to measure 1 cup. Place the empty, lifeless carcasses of the tomatoes (or the bell peppers) in the prepared baking dish.

3 In a large sauté pan or soup pot, warm the oil over medium-high heat. Add the onions and sauté them around until they start to get a little golden brown, 5 to 8 minutes. Add the tomato guts (if using tomatoes), garlic, oregano, thyme, pepper flakes, salt, and black pepper and mix all that shit up for about 1 minute. Stir in the rice and broth (use 1¾ cups if you're stuffing peppers).

4 Bring the pan to a simmer, then cover, reduce the heat to low, and cook until all the liquid has been absorbed and the rice is tender, 15 minutes for white or 25 minutes for brown rice.

5 Meanwhile, crank the oven to 400°F.

6 When the rice is done, remove from the heat and fold in the chickpeas, lemon juice, parsley, and mint. Taste and add more of whateverthefuck you think it needs.

7 Fill the tomatoes or peppers generously with the rice filling, kinda packing it down to make sure they're full, and place the cut-off tops back on. Did ya accidentally throw the tops away because you broke our first rule of cooking and didn't read the whole recipe first? Bet you microwave something and hafta dig the box outta the trash, too. This is clearly a you problem but not a deal breaker.

8 Drizzle the tops with some more olive oil, cover the baking dish with the lid or foil, and bake until the tomatoes or peppers look tender and starting to brown in some spots, 30 to 45 minutes for tomatoes and probably at least 15 minutes longer for the peppers. Serve right away with some extra chopped fresh parsley or mint on top if you're into presentation.

* If using bell peppers, the broth is increased to 1¾ cups to offset the lack of tomato guts. Also the baking time is extended by at least 15 minutes, 'cause those fuckers are sturdier.

COOK TIME 25 MIN

》Makes enough for 4 people

DRESSING

½ cup rice vinegar

1 tablespoon mirin, apple juice, or your favorite liquid sweetener

2 tablespoons tahini

2 tablespoons toasted sesame oil

2 tablespoons grapeseed or other neutral oil

1 clove garlic, chopped

1 tablespoon minced fresh ginger

1 tablespoon soy sauce or tamari

NOODLES

16 ounces soba or udon noodles

2 cups frozen shelled edamame*

½ cucumber, cut into matchsticks

1 carrot, cut into matchsticks

1 bell pepper or other sweet pepper, cut into matchsticks

⅓ cup chopped watercress**

¼ cup sliced green onions

Sesame seeds

This recipe is more of a building block than anything, so modify this shit however you like. We're just giving you the foundation for you to build your favorite kinda bowl. Watercress is kinda peppery and if you can't find it, just sub in arugula or cilantro. This is great when there's almost nothing in the fridge. You can toss on our Lemongrass Baked Tofu (page 122) and jazz that bitch up.

SIMPLE SESAME NOODLES WITH EDAMAME AND WATERCRESS

1 First make the dressing: Add all the ingredients to a blender or food processor. Run until everything is mixed and the ginger is basically destroyed. Set this aside.

2 When you're ready to eat, make the noodles: Cook them according to the package directions. About a minute before they're done, throw in the edamame so that they can thaw and soften up. This is legit the laziest way to blanch veggies, so feel free to use this tip for asparagus, kale, or whatever you wanna eat with some noodles. When the noodles are done, drain the noodles and edamame in a colander, and run them under some cold water to cool 'em off.

3 Throw the cooled noodles and edamame into a large bowl. Add all the veggie matchsticks, the watercress, and green onions. Add about three-quarters of the dressing and mix all that together until everything is coated in dressing and all mixed up.

4 You can either serve this right away or you can let this cool for a couple hours in the fridge. When you're ready to serve this shit, pour in the remaining dressing, and toss again to freshen that fucker up. Garnish with sesame seeds.

* You can find these in the freezer section near the other frozen veggies.

** Hate watercress or can't find it? Sub in cilantro, basil, mint, or a mix.

TWILIGHT TREATS

DESSERTS & DRINKS

Banana Date Shake 148

Mulled Spiked Apple Cider 149

Strawberry Rosewater Cheesecake 150

Fig And Ginger Fizz Punch 152

Green Grape Pie 155

Grapefruit Cake 158

Agua Fresca 159

Mezcal Meltdown 161

Orangesicle Bars 162

Plum-Side-Down Cake 165

Fresh Peach Pudding 166

Kiwi Colada 167

The Gincident Cocktail 168

Peach And Pear Pie 170

Winter Squash Blondies 172

Zucchini Bundt Cake 173

Peanut Better Cookies 175

BRAVE
NEW
MEAL

BAD
MANNERS

BRAVE
NEW MEAL

BY BAD MANNERS

» Makes
2 shakes

3 bananas,* chopped
(preferably frozen but
not a deal breaker)

¼ cup almond,
cashew, or peanut
butter

4 to 6 dates,** pitted
and chopped*

¼ teaspoon ground
cinnamon, plus more
for sprinkling

2¼ cups vanilla
nondairy milk

Palm Springs, California, is famous for two things: being hotter than Satan's asshole and the birthplace of the date shake. It's a tasty summertime treat whose creation was inspired by survival more than anything else. So next time it feels oppressively hot, activate your internal AC with this banana date shake.

BANANA DATE SHAKE

Throw all that shit in a blender and blend the fuck out of it until it's all creamy with no chunks. Chunks are good sometimes. Stews? Hell, yeah, chunk it up. Shakes? CREAMY, BITCH. Add more milk or less depending on how thick you like it. Serve with a sprinkle of cinnamon on top.

Don't know about banana clones and this fruit's crazy life? Learn all about 'em on page 220.

** The number of dates you add will depend on how fresh and plump your dates are and how sweet you like it. You do YOU.

Dates are the fruit from certain kinds of palm trees, and you can find them dried near the nuts at your grocery store. They have an almost caramel taste that's not to be missed. If you live in place that has palm trees, you can probably get these sweet sons of bitches at your farmer's market, where they'll be extra fresh. Store 'em in the fridge when you get home to help them last a few extra months.

A classic winter treat that's tasty, cheap as hell, and all ya hafta do is boil some stuff. Perfect lazy choice for your next family get-together when do you don't wanna cook shit. Easy cop-out when you say you're gonna bring somethin'.

MULLED SPIKED APPLE CIDER

» Makes enough for 4 to 6 people

1 In a large pot, combine the cider, orange peel, ginger, cinnamon sticks, cloves, and star anise and bring to a simmer over medium heat. Reduce the heat to medium-low and let it simmer for 30 minutes to 1 hour to make sure all the spices have time to flavor that juice up. When it tastes good to you, add the brandy, then remove from the heat.

2 Let this sweet winter bastard cool for a few minutes, then fish out the orange, ginger slices, and spices (or don't and just let the people deal with it, up to you). Serve hot. We're extra lazy and just stick a ladle in the pot, but you can put it in mugs for people if you really want. Top with some coconut whipped cream if that sounds like something you might be into.

* Just grab what looks legit. We like unfiltered apple juice, which is usually labeled "cider" depending on where you're at. Don't grab hard apple cider though, that shit is way different.

** This is a cool as fuck spice but can be hard to find. Don't have it at your store? Leave it out.

*** Driving the sleigh tonight? You can leave this out.

6 cups apple cider or juice*

1 thumb-size piece of orange peel

5 quarter-size slices fresh ginger

3 cinnamon sticks

1 tablespoon whole cloves

3 whole star anise**

1 cup brandy or bourbon***

Coconut Milk Whipped Cream (optional; page 189)

>> **Makes one cheesecake, enough for 8 to 12 people**

CRUST

1½ cups vanilla cookie crumbs*

3 tablespoons cane sugar

⅓ cup nondairy butter or coconut oil, melted

FILLING

3 cups cashews, soaked in warm water for 2 hours (annoying, we know)

¾ cup unsweetened finely shredded coconut

1 cup brown rice syrup**

1 cup refined coconut oil

2 tablespoons fresh lemon juice

2 to 4 tablespoons rose water***

2½ cups chopped strawberries****

The blender does all the work here so if you can press "blend" and pour, then this is your shit. Say hello to your new signature dessert. If strawberries are out of season, try the passion fruit version for a really decadent and fancy-as-fuck treat.

STRAWBERRY ROSEWATER CHEESECAKE

1 Preheat the oven to 375°F. Grab a 9-inch springform pan.

2 Make the crust: In a small bowl, mix the cookie crumbs, sugar, and melted butter until everything is incorporated. Press this firmly onto the bottom of the springform so it looks like a crust. You know how. Now bake this empty motherfucker for 15 minutes so that it can firm up and get a little golden.

3 While that shit is baking, make the filling: Drain and rinse the cashews and add to a blender along with the coconut, brown rice syrup, and coconut oil and let that shit go until it looks pretty smooth. Add the lemon juice, rose water, and strawberries and run that shit again until it's smooth like peanut butter in there.

4 Pour this into the baked crust and stick that fucker in the fridge overnight to get nice and firm. This is a thicc boy, so it's gonna take a few hours. That's it, though. Done.

5 After it's set, slice and serve with some fresh berries on top.

* Use whatever kind of vanilla or plain shortbread, sugar, or wafer cookies you like and just throw them in the blender or food processor until you've got crumbs.

** This is an old-school hippie ingredient that will be near the honey in the grocery store. It's thick like molasses but not as sweet as maple syrup. It's perfect in shit like this because it sweetens, holds stuff together, and doesn't make everything too watery.

To make this a tropical treat leave out the strawberries and rose water, and sub in 2 cups chopped mango, fresh or frozen. Blend the mango in when you'd add the strawberries, then stir in ½ cup of our Passion Fruit Preserves (page 191). Pour another ½ cup of the passion fruit preserves over the baked crust before you pour in the blended filling. Chill like above and top with any remaining preserves or fresh passion fruit.

*** If you've never cooked with rose water before, start with the smallest measurement and add more if you like how it tastes in the filling. Don't use some shitty rose water face spray here with god-knows-what kind of weird shit in it. Grab food-grade rose water, which should be near either the vanilla extract or falafel mix in the store.

**** You could def substitute in another berry like raspberries or even cherries, but use 2 cups of fruit instead. If you use blackberries, leave out the rose water and try orange blossom water instead.

COOK TIME
30 MIN

》 **Makes enough for 4 to 6 people**

10 fresh figs*

½ cup Ginger Simple Syrup (recipe follows)

2 sprigs of fresh thyme

1 bottle (750ml) dry champagne or bubbly lemon-lime soda

½ cup gin

Crushed ice

* Learn more about figs on page 234 so you don't fuck this up.

Punch is for when you know you're gonna want more than one drink but you don't wanna keep getting up and making them. This punch is gorgeous and delicious, and will get the drinking job done in style. Cheers, bitches.

FIG AND GINGER FIZZ PUNCH

1 Slice all the figs in half lengthwise, setting 2 aside for later.

2 In a small saucepan, bring the ginger simple syrup, sliced figs, and thyme to a simmer over low heat. Slowly simmer, stirring often, until the figs have started to soften, about 8 minutes. Remove from the heat and let this mixture sit for about 5 minutes so the thyme can infuse the mixture. Once the syrupy mix has cooled a little, pull out the thyme.

3 Grab a food processor, blender, or immersion blender and blend up the softened figs and ginger simple syrup until it's smooth. Yeah, the fig seeds are still gonna be in there, but you don't want any fucking chunks, okay?

4 In a large pitcher, mix together the champagne and gin. Stir in the ginger-fig syrup and add a good amount of crushed ice and reserved figs—so people know what the fuck is going on—and enjoy.

» **Makes about ⅔ cup**

½ cup water
½ cup cane sugar
¼ cup peeled and
sliced fresh ginger*

*Learn more about this
tasty-as-fuck root on
page 235.*

GINGER SIMPLE SYRUP

This is basically an amped-up simple syrup which
you can add to cocktails, lemonade, agua fresca,
or even a fruit salad to spice that shit up. No
ginger? Try it with a couple big slices of orange
or lemon zest, a couple sprigs of rosemary, or
whatever the fuck sounds good to you.

In a small saucepan, bring the water, sugar, and ginger to a
boil over medium-high heat. Reduce the heat and let that
shit simmer for 8 to 10 minutes until it starts to thicken up
and reduce. Stir every couple minutes to make sure none of
the sugary water is clumping on the sides. Once it is looking
thicker, turn off the heat and fish out the ginger slices. Let that
shit cool then stick it in a jar in your fridge. It should last in
there for at least a week.

Grape pies are hard as hell to find and we can't figure out why. Sure, they might look a lil weird at first, but one bite and you are hooked.

GREEN GRAPE PIE

1 Warm up the oven to 425°F.

2 Roll out one pie crust and then fit it into a 9-inch pie pan. Line the bottom of the crust with an even layer of the minced walnuts, then place the pie pan in the freezer while you prep the filling.

3 In your largest skillet or sauté pan (big enough to hold the grapes in a single layer), combine the grapes, sugar, cinnamon, nutmeg, lemon juice, and maple syrup. Set over medium heat and cook until the grapes are all warmed up and some of the skins start fallin' off, about 8 minutes.

4 Add the orange blossom water and salt, then stir in the cornstarch, making sure it dissolves and doesn't clump. Keep simmering and stirring, until the mixture has thickened slightly, about 3 more minutes.

5 Remove the skillet from the heat and stir in the tapioca flour, making sure it all dissolves. Let that sit for about 5 minutes while you roll out your top crust. After sitting the mixture should be a lil thicker.

6 Using a slotted spoon, remove the grapes from the liquid and place them in the already prepped pie pan with the walnut layer. Use a measuring cup and scoop ½ cup outta the skillet liquid, then pour that shit over the grapes in the pie pan. This is just enough to make the pie moist but not runny. (Whatever juice is left in the skillet can be thrown out, or drink it if you're a fucking maniac, but save a bit for brushing the top of the crust in the next step.)

COOK TIME
80 MIN

》 **Makes one 9-inch pie, enough for 8 people or 1 lonely motherfucker**

2 unbaked pie crusts (page 188)

1 cup minced walnuts

2 pounds green grapes (about 7 cups once you take them off the stems)

¾ cup sugar, plus more for sprinkling

¼ teaspoon ground cinnamon

¼ teaspoon ground nutmeg

Juice of 1 lemon (about 2 tablespoons)

¼ cup pure maple syrup

1 tablespoon orange blossom water*

¼ teaspoon salt

3 tablespoons cornstarch

2 tablespoons tapioca flour

Optional but fucking delicious.

(continued)

7 Press the second rolled-out crust on top of the pan and crimp the edges together. Brush the crust with a bit of the remaining pan juice, then sprinkle it with a little sugar. Cut a few small slits in the top to let some of the steam out while it bakes. You can draw dicks, we don't care, the pie just needs to breathe.

8 Bake until the crust is golden brown, 30 to 40 minutes. Let cool completely before serving. This pie is great to make a day ahead 'cause it's even better the next day when it's been soakin' for a while.

Orange blossom water is a by-product of making bitter orange essential oil and has been used in food and drinks for centuries. It's fucking delicious and one bottle will last you awhile. Add a splash to your favorite cocktail or lemonade on a hot day and people will think you're a goddamn genius. Look for it near the extracts in the baking aisle or near the tahini and falafel mix at the grocery store. Can't find it? Leave it out.

»Makes one 8-inch cake

CAKE

Coconut oil or nondairy butter, for the pan

1¼ cups unbleached all-purpose flour, plus more for the pan

¼ cup semolina, cornmeal, or almond flour

1 teaspoon baking powder

½ teaspoon baking soda

½ teaspoon salt

1 teaspoon grated grapefruit zest

½ cup sugar

¼ cup freshly squeezed grapefruit juice

1 teaspoon vanilla extract

¼ cup almond milk

¼ cup olive oil

1 cup nondairy yogurt

GLAZE

¼ cup chopped grapefruit flesh

¼ cup freshly squeezed grapefruit juice, plus extra for the cornstarch

2 tablespoons cane sugar

1 teaspoon cornstarch

People either love or hate grapefruit, but everyone loves cake, making this the great unifier our country needs right now.

GRAPEFRUIT CAKE

1 Warm up the oven to 350°F. Grease and flour an 8-inch cake pan with coconut oil or your favorite nondairy butter.

2 Make the cake: In a medium bowl, mix the all-purpose flour, semolina, baking powder, baking soda, and salt.

3 In a large bowl, combine the zest and sugar and rub them together with your fingers until no chunks of zest are left. Stir in the grapefruit juice, vanilla, milk, olive oil, and yogurt. Add the flour to the wet mixture and stir until there are no big lumps.

4 Pour the batter into the prepared cake pan and bake until the top is golden and a toothpick stuck in the cake comes out clean, 30 to 40 minutes. Let the cake cool in the pan for 15 minutes.

5 While that fucker is cooling, make the glaze: In a small saucepan, combine the flesh, juice, and sugar and heat over medium heat. Stir until all the sugar has dissolved. In a small glass, mix together the cornstarch and just a little grapefruit juice until the cornstarch has dissolved. Pour this slurry into the pan and stir until the glaze starts to thicken, then remove from the heat.

6 When the cake has cooled, take it out of the pan, place it on a plate, and pour the glaze over it. Serve right away.

This shit right here is nature's Kool-Aid. Throw in your favorite fruit and blend up your new favorite drink in no time flat.

AGUA FRESCA

1 Toss all the ingredients in a blender and run it. If your fruit isn't super sweet, add more agave to get it where you like it. Fucking DONE. Unless your blender is small, then do this shit in batches and combine it in one big-ass jug. Some people strain the blended fruit for pulp, which makes the consistency a bit more watery. Not us, we like pulp in that motherfucker. Every sip is a reminder you're drinking goddamn fruit instead of fake fruit bullshit. Now you're really fucking done.

2 This is best the day it's made, but it will keep for 3 days or so in the fridge. Just stir that shit to redistribute all that pulpy goodness before you sip.

* We like cantaloupe, but this shit is very open to interpretation depending on what you can get and what's in season. Fucking delicious substitutions include: watermelon, honeydew melon, any other sweet summer melon, strawberries, pineapple, and mango. You can do a mix, too, or add a cucumber or a sprig or two of mint and make something that's all your own. And yeah, frozen fruit works here too. Depending on what fruit you use and your own taste buds, you may need more or less sugar than the recipe calls for.

COOK TIME 10 MIN

» **Makes enough for 4 to 6 people, depending on your pour**

6 cups chunks of fruit*

4 cups water

1 cup ice

¼ cup lime juice (2 to 3 limes)

2 to 4 tablespoons agave or cane sugar

Pinch of salt

SOMEWHERE BETWEEN VACATION AND THERAPY

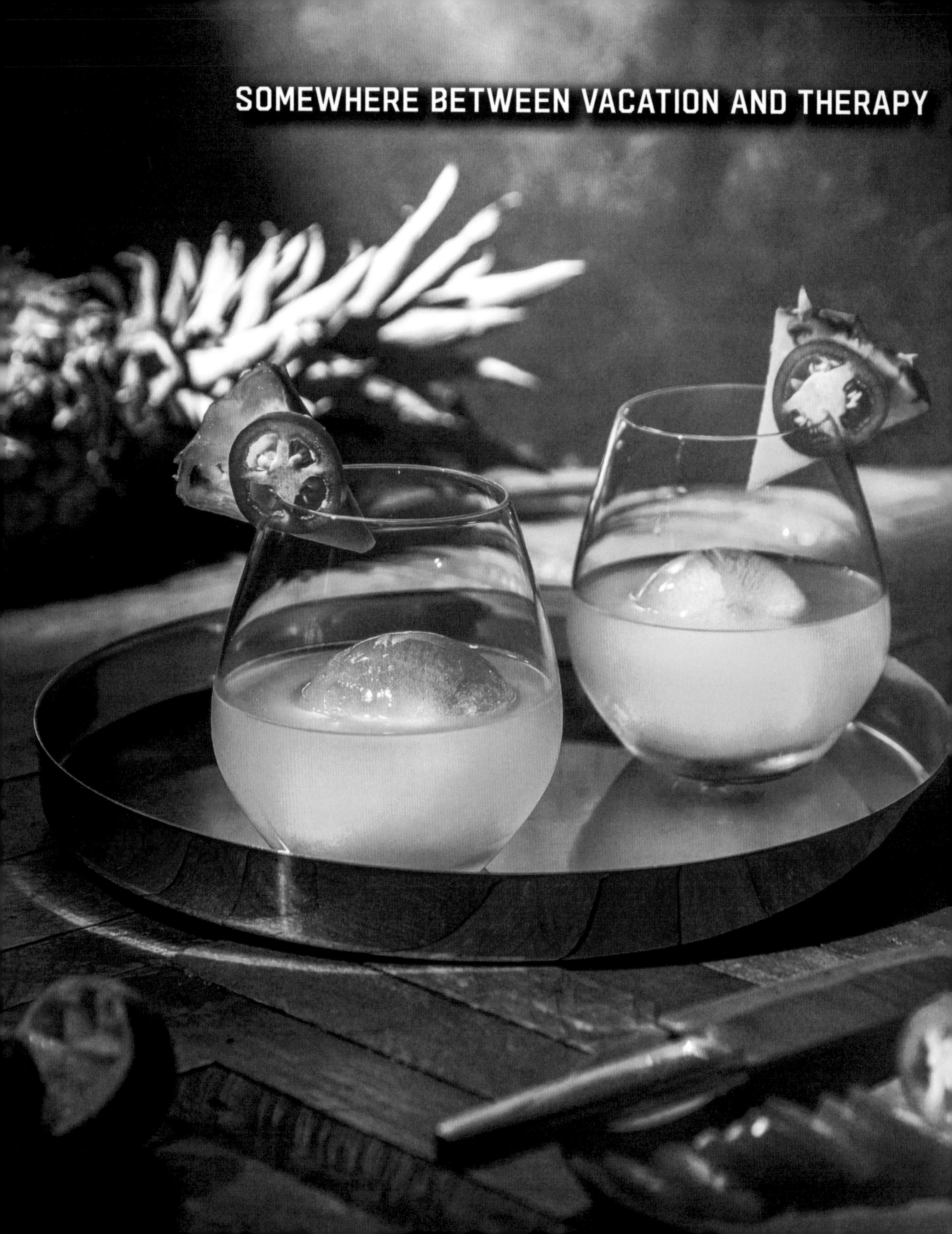

Smoky mezcal was made for pineapple juice. They complement each other so well it's hard to imagine one without the other, like chips and guac. Milk and cookies. Picard and Data. What the fuck were we talking about? Oh yeah, a cocktail.

MEZCAL MELTDOWN

1 Grab a jar with a tight-fitting lid. Fill it with some ice then add the mezcal, jalapeno, and lime juice. Shake the fuck out of it until everything is cold and the jalapeno is all mashed up.

2 Get two largish glasses and fill them with ice. Divide the pineapple juice between the two glasses then strain the shaker into them evenly. You don't want any jalapeño pieces floatin' around in there. Well, at least we fucking don't. Serve immediately.

COOK TIME 5 MIN

» **Makes 2 cocktails**

Ice

½ cup mezcal

1 small jalapeño, thinly sliced

½ cup freshly squeezed lime juice

1 cup pineapple juice

**›› Makes about
9 bars, depending on
how you slice shit**

OAT BASE

1½ cups rolled oats

3 tablespoons almond butter

3 tablespoons coconut oil

¼ cup brown sugar

1 teaspoon baking soda

1 teaspoon vanilla extract

¼ teaspoon salt

ORANGESICLE FILLING

1½ cups unsweetened finely shredded coconut*

1 cup coconut cream**

Grated zest of 1 large orange (about 1 tablespoon)

1 cup freshly squeezed orange juice (a little pulp is fine)

¼ cup pure maple syrup

¼ cup cornstarch or arrowroot powder

½ teaspoon vanilla extract

¼ teaspoon salt

Coconut Milk Whipped Cream (optional, page 189)

This is a cross between an ice cream bar and a cream pie. So basically heaven.

ORANGESICLE BARS

1 Warm up the oven to 350°F. Grease an 8-inch square baking dish, then line it with parchment paper.

2 Make the oat base: In a food processor, combine the oats, almond butter, coconut oil, brown sugar, baking soda, vanilla, and salt. Pulse that shit for a few seconds until there aren't any whole oats but that shit is still a little coarser than flour. Scoop that mixture out and press it in an even layer into the prepared pan. Not like get-out-a-level kind of even, just try a little.

3 Throw this empty crust into the oven and bake until it doesn't look so fucking raw anymore and the edges start to cook and look just a little golden, 8 to 12 minutes.

4 Meanwhile, make the filling: In a blender, combine the shredded coconut, coconut cream, orange zest, orange juice, maple syrup, cornstarch, vanilla, and salt and run that shit until the filling is smooth and creamy as hell.

5 When the crust is done, pour the filling into the crust and try to make it an even layer. Don't get lazy this far in. Throw back in the oven and bake until the top doesn't look super wet and the pan doesn't jiggle a ton when you hit the side of the dish, 15 to 20 minutes. Jiggling like Jell-O? Keep baking.

6 Let this cool on the counter to room temp. We like them a few hours after they've been in the fridge 'cause then they're extra firm, but we get it if you can't wait. When you serve them, top with coconut whipped cream or an orange slice.

* This unsweetened stuff should be in the baking aisle in your store.

** This is that hardened, thick part that separates from the thinner coconut milk when it's been sitting awhile. They sell cans of just the cream too, so use what you've got.

THE ONLY BAR THAT NEVER CLOSES

FROSTING
CAN'T FUCK WITH
FRUIT

In terms of stone fruits, peaches seem to get all the attention, but plums are just as fucking delicious when it comes to desserts.

PLUM-SIDE-DOWN CAKE

1 Warm the oven to 350°F then grease and flour a 9-inch cake pan. Put a round of parchment paper in the bottom of the pan and grease and flour that too. That's cake insurance, baby.

2 In a small saucepan, heat the butter and brown sugar over medium-low heat. Warm that up until the butter has melted and the sugar has dissolved, 3 to 4 minutes. When it looks all caramelly, pour this into the prepared cake pan. Carefully arrange the plum wedges in the caramel in whatever cool-as-fuck pattern you can manage.

3 Now let's batter the fuck up. In a large bowl, mix together the olive oil and granulated sugar until well combined and the sugar kinda starts to dissolve, about 1 minute of whisking. Add the baking soda, baking powder, and salt and whisk again. Add the vanilla and almond extracts, vinegar, and milk and mix again until smooth and kinda creamy, about a minute of whisking. Consider it the workout you want to justify having an extra slice of cake.

4 Now add the flour in four batches so that you can mix it all in without a shit-ton of clumps. When the batter is ready to go, pour it over the plum slices as evenly as you can. Bake for 40 to 55 minutes, until the top looks golden and a toothpick stuck in the center comes out clean.

5 Now the hardest part: waiting. Let the cake cool in the pan for 30 minutes and then invert the cake onto a big plate so that the plums are on the top. Pull off the parchment and boom, pretty cake reveal. Let it cool completely then serve with ice cream or our whipped cream (page 189).

COOK TIME
115 MIN

>> **Makes 1 cake, enough for 1 to 10 people, depending on your lifestyle**

¼ cup nondairy butter

½ cup brown sugar

3 plums, pitted and cut into ½-inch-thick wedges*

½ cup olive oil

1 cup granulated sugar

½ teaspoon baking soda

½ teaspoon baking powder

½ teaspoon salt

1 teaspoon vanilla extract

1 teaspoon almond extract

1 teaspoon apple cider vinegar

1 cup nondairy milk

2 cups all-purpose flour

*No plums? Any stone fruit would do. You can use peaches, nectarines, apricots, whatever you can find. Nothing fresh? Frozen peach slices would be fine here too, just defrost them before adding them to the pan.

COOK TIME 25 MIN

>> **Makes enough for 4 people**

1½ cups (1 can) full-fat coconut milk

1 cup almond milk

2 cups peach puree (about 4 peaches, pitted, chopped, and pureed in a food processor), plus more for serving

¼ cup cornstarch or arrowroot powder

5 tablespoons pure maple syrup

1 teaspoon vanilla extract

¼ teaspoon salt

Coconut Milk Whipped Cream (optional; page 189)

Other than being an excellent stage name, this is a quick and simple dessert. Ya just need time to chill it in the fridge to set. You are not only capable of making, but dammit you deserve, some fresh peach pudding.

FRESH PEACH PUDDING

1 Grab a large saucepan and add the coconut milk, almond milk, peach puree, and cornstarch. Whisk that shit, making sure the cornstarch isn't all clumpy. Cook over medium heat until bubbling and thickened, about 5 minutes. You're going for pudding texture. Duh.

2 Turn off the heat and stir in the maple syrup, vanilla, and salt. If your peaches weren't super sweet, add more maple syrup as needed. Pour this into a nonmetal bowl and let it chill on the counter for about 15 minutes. After it's cooled down a little, cover the bowl with plastic wrap or parchment paper so that it touches the surface of the pudding to prevent the dreaded pudding skin. Fucking disgusting.

3 Refrigerate for a couple hours or overnight so it can thicken up. Serve as is or topped with coconut whipped cream and more sliced peaches.

Do you like hairy small fruits and gettin' caught in the rain? Well, we've got you covered on the first part. Just drink it standing in the shower and you're all set.

KIWI COLADA

Throw everything in a blender that can fucking handle some ice and let that shit run until your drink is as smooth as you imagine yourself being after you drink it. Taste and add more sweetener if your kiwi weren't ripe enough. Garnish it with a slice of kiwi on the rim if you wanna look fancy.

* Or you know, whatever amount you want based on how shitty your day was using what rum you got. No judgment here. Not drinking? Substitute water, more coconut milk, or coconut water for a chill treat without the kick.

** You can totally leave this out if you don't like your drinks sweet. But we say fucking go for it. You earned it.

COOK TIME
5 MIN

» **Makes enough for 4 to 6 people, depending on how fucked up you plan to get**

6 kiwis, peeled and cut into slices (save some slices for garnish)

2 cups ice cubes

1½ cups frozen pineapple chunks

1½ cups pineapple juice

¾ cup white rum*

½ cup canned full-fat coconut milk

2 tablespoons fresh lime juice

2 tablespoons agave or your favorite liquid sweetener**

>> Makes 2
cocktails

Ice

6 thick slices
cucumber, skin on
or off

4 fresh mint or basil
leaves, torn up*

½ cup of your
favorite gin

2 tablespoons fresh
lime juice

1 tablespoon agave or
pure maple syrup

1 cup ginger beer**

Life is dumb and hard. But it gets a little better
when you can reward yourself for getting through
the bullshit with a drink after a long-ass day.

THE GINCIDENT COCKTAIL

1 Grab a jar with a tight-fitting lid. Fill it with some ice then
add the cucumber, mint if you're using it, gin, lime juice, and
the agave. Shake the fuck out of it until everything is cold and
the cucumber and mint are all bashed up and releasing their
flavors.

2 Get two largish glasses and fill them with ice. Divide the
ginger beer between the two glasses then strain the shaker into
both glasses, trying to keep that shit even. Serve right away.

* Optional but you're worth the fucking effort.

** Ginger beer is best, but if you don't have it a lemon-lime soda or flavored
soda water will work too.

SPECIAL

OCCASION

SAUCE

**》 Makes one
9-inch pie, you
do the math**

1 unbaked pie crust
(page 188)

10 saltine crackers,
crumbled

½ cup nondairy milk
or water

3 tablespoons
nondairy butter or
coconut oil

1 cup cane sugar

¼ cup packed brown
sugar

¼ cup pure maple
syrup

1 tablespoon vanilla
extract

1 firm-ripe pear,
chopped into
bite-size bits

3 tablespoons
cornstarch or tapioca
flour

½ teaspoon salt

¼ teaspoon ground
cinnamon

1½ cups pecan halves,
toasted (see page 46)

Coconut Milk
Whipped Cream
(page 189) or vanilla
ice cream, for serving

This delicious mash-up of some of our favorite pies. You might wanna say it's a frankenpie, but technically it'd be a monster dessert created by Chef Frankenstein. He was the creator not the creation, ya understand? Yeah us neither, just grab a pitchfork and dig in. But maybe make it the day before you want to eat it so you can see it at its best.

PECAN AND PEAR PIE

1 Crank your oven to 425°F.

2 Fit the pie crust into a 9-inch pie pan. Trim and shape the edges (pinch or crimp them using a fork). Prick the crust bottom with a fork, then line the crust with parchment and throw in some dried beans you don't care about. We're blind baking this bitch and need to hold the crust down. Stick this in the oven and bake for 15 minutes. Just so the bottom doesn't look all raw. Take it out, turn the heat down to 350°F, and set that crust aside while we make our filling. And yeah, obviously remove the beans and parchment. Just wait until that shit isn't crazy hot.

3 In a small bowl, stir together the crackers and milk. It's like a super-sad cereal. Let that sit for 5 minutes so it gets a little paste-like.

4 Grab a food processor or blender and throw in the cracker paste (yum), butter, both sugars, the maple syrup, vanilla, half of the chopped pear, the cornstarch, salt, and cinnamon. Let that shit run until it looks mostly smooth and there aren't a bunch of cornstarch blobs floating around in there.

5 Grab a medium saucepan and pour in your sugar slurry from the food processor. Bring that sweet shit to a simmer over medium-high heat, then cook until all the sugar has dissolved and it's starting to thicken up a little, about 3 minutes longer.

Just don't let that sugar start to burn, so wait until this fucker goes in the oven to check IG. Fold in the pecans, make sure they're all coated, then remove from the heat.

6 Fill the partially baked pie crust with the remaining pear and then pour in the pecan filling. Try to even it out with the back of a spoon so it looks presentable and shit. Brush the edges of the crust with a little nondairy milk and return to the oven to bake until the crust is browned and the filling doesn't look super wet and doesn't jiggle when you gentle hit the side of the pan, 40 to 50 minutes.

7 When it's done you gotta let this fucker cool for hours, ideally overnight, to make sure the filling has time to set and not be all runny and sad. Sure, it's still tasty as fuck if it's runny but not at all impressive. Have some patience.

8 Slice and serve as with some whipped coconut cream or vanilla ice cream.

COOK TIME 80 MIN

» **Makes one 8-inch square pan**

⅓ **cup crystallized ginger***

⅓ **cup chopped toasted walnuts, pecans, or almonds****

2 tablespoons ground flaxseeds

¼ **cup almond or other nondairy milk**

⅓ **cup olive oil**

⅔ **cup cane sugar**

1 cup winter squash puree***

2 teaspoons vanilla extract

1¼ **cups whole wheat pastry flour or all-purpose flour**

½ **teaspoon baking powder**

½ **teaspoon salt**

½ **teaspoon ground cinnamon**

¼ **teaspoon ground ginger**

Can't find? Use chocolate or peanut butter chips.

** *See How to Toast Nuts, page 46.*

*** *Just peel, chop up, and steam a sweet-fleshed squash until tender and toss in the blender, or use canned pumpkin if that's what you've got.*

We know what you're thinking: blondies are a dessert. Why would anyone put squash in a dessert? Well, guess what? PUMPKIN FUCKING PIE. Now stop with all those preconceived notions and go read up on winter squashes on page 247. Then let's get baking, bitch.

WINTER SQUASH BLONDIES

1 Crank up the oven to 350°F. Grease and flour an 8-inch square baking dish, ya know, the brownie pan.

2 Cut up the ginger and nuts into bite-size pieces. Aim for the size of a chocolate chip for each ingredient. In a small glass, stir together the flaxseeds and milk, then set that shit aside.

3 In a medium bowl, mix together the oil, sugar, squash puree, and vanilla until everything's all incorporated and there aren't any dry sugar pockets. In another bowl, whisk together the flour, baking powder, salt, cinnamon, and ground ginger.

4 Now add the squash mixture and flaxseed/milk mixture to the flour bowl and mix that motherfucker up until there aren't any more clumps of flour. Yeah, the batter is gonna be thick, don't worry you didn't fuck anything up. Fold in the ginger and walnuts. If you want to be fancy, save some of those to stick on top so the blondies look all legit and kinda decorated.

5 Pour the batter into the baking dish. You're gonna need to spread it around with a spatula or the back of a spoon to get that shit nice and even because that fucker won't spread on its own. If you left any walnuts or ginger out, gently press those onto the top and that shit will look artisan as fuck.

6 Bake it until a toothpick comes out clean, 35 to 45 minutes. Let it cool in the pan for at least 20 minutes before cutting into bars and serving.

Your polite but overly friendly neighbor just gave you a shitload of zucchini you didn't ask for. Now, normally a plant-based cookbook would tell you to spiralize them into faux noodles, but we're gonna suggest you bake those bitches into a Bundt. Great way to deal with excess zucchini, especially if you're looking to trick kids into eating their veggies—just use cake. Learn more about summer squash on page 246.

ZUCCHINI BUNDT CAKE

1 Warm up the oven to 375°F. Grease and flour a Bundt pan.

2 In a medium bowl, mix together the zucchini, banana, oil, yogurt, milk, lemon juice, and vanilla. Stir so everything is incorporated and there aren't giant zucchini clumps in there.

3 In a large bowl, whisk together the flour, both sugars, the baking soda, salt, and spices. Make a well in the center of the flour mixture and pour in the zucchini mixture. Stir this up until everything is just combined and there aren't any big-ass dry spots of flour. Fold in the nuts.

4 Pour the batter into that Bundt pan from earlier. Bake until toothpick stuck in the cake comes out clean, about 45 minutes.

5 Let cool in the pan for 15 minutes, then flip that shit over onto a rack or plate to cool for at least 30 more minutes so the cake has a chance to firm up. Taste this shit too early and it will feel all gummy in your mouth and make you sad.

6 It will keep for about 5 days but it won't last that long if anyone in your house has working taste buds.

* Use the side of your box grater, you know that thing you use for cheese, or if you are super fucking lazy, the grater on your food processor.

** Can't find this/don't want to buy it? Just use more cinnamon instead.

*** For instructions on toasting nuts, see page 46.

COOK TIME 90 MIN

》Makes 1 standard Bundt cake

2½ cups grated* zucchini (about 3 good-size zucchini) or other soft summer squash

2 bananas, mashed well

½ cup olive oil

¾ cup plain or vanilla nondairy yogurt

½ cup nondairy milk

1 tablespoon fresh lemon juice

2 teaspoons vanilla extract

2¾ cups whole wheat pastry or all-purpose flour

½ cup cane sugar

¼ cup brown sugar

1 teaspoon baking soda

½ teaspoon salt

1 teaspoon ground cinnamon

½ teaspoon ground cardamom**

½ teaspoon ground ginger

¼ teaspoon ground nutmeg**

1 cup chopped toasted walnuts or pecans***

CLASSICS ARE ALWAYS IN SEASON

A classic peanut butter cookie without all the butter and way less sugar. Get your fix without all the bullshit. Wanna really treat yourself? Serve these with our Banana Date Shakes (page 148) and you'll forget all about whatever was stressing you out for at least 15 minutes.

COOK TIME
60 MIN

» Makes 24 cookies

2 cups all-purpose flour or whole wheat pastry flour

1 teaspoon baking soda

1 teaspoon salt

1 cup smooth or chunky peanut butter, your call

½ cup pure maple syrup

½ cup packed brown sugar

¼ cup olive oil

⅓ cup almond milk

1½ teaspoons vanilla extract

PEANUT BETTER COOKIES

1 In a medium bowl, mix together the flour, baking soda, and salt. In a large bowl, combine the peanut butter, maple syrup, brown sugar, olive oil, almond milk, and vanilla. Stir until this is all mixed up and there aren't any dry sugar clumps floating around in there. Pour the flour mixture in the peanut butter bowl and stir until barely combined. This batter is thick as fuck, we know. You just gotta give it a little of time to get its shit straight, so stick it in the fridge for 30 minutes or up to overnight before baking.

2 When you're ready to bake, warm up your oven to 350°F and line two baking sheets with parchment paper.

3 To prepare the cookies, make balls using 2 to 3 tablespoons of the dough. Place them on the prepared baking sheets. Press down on each one with the back of a fork to get that classic peanut butter cookie look. You know you wanna.

4 Bake for 10 to 12 minutes, until they are just getting golden on the bottom and firming up. Let them cool on the baking sheet for a couple minutes before moving them over to a cooling rack or into your fucking mouth.

KITCHEN CREDO

EL CAMINO
MARKET
NO MASK, NO SERVICE!

EVERYDAY STAPLES

Back here we've got all the basics you need to start creating your own damn recipes from scratch. Whether you're looking up how to cook the perfect pot of rice, how to make some pizza dough, blend up a pesto, or throw together a salad dressing, we've got all your go-to shit right here. So read on up and start getting creative now that you've got foundation foods locked down.

✱ HOW TO PREPARE GRAINS

Cooking grains tends to go quicker than cooking beans, but these motherfuckers require a little more maintenance. Just like beans, know that they're gonna double in volume when you cook 'em, so 1 cup of uncooked rice will give you 2 cups cooked. Use the following guides to get some grains going, just be sure to adjust that shit for how much you need for whatever you're making. If you ever end up with extra water in the pot when your grains are done, just drain that shit off. You don't wanna cook until the grains are all mushy. Also, if you run out of water and your grains aren't done, just pour more in. You're not gonna fuck anything up. You got this. FUCKING BELIEVE IN YOURSELF. WE BELIEVE IN YOU AND WE'VE NEVER EVEN MET.

BARLEY

This grain is nutty, chewy, and highly underrated. Not only is it full of fiber, but it's packed with selenium, copper, and manganese so you know you're getting your money's worth. There are two main kinds of barley you're gonna run into at the store: hulled and pearled. Hulled takes longer to cook but has more fiber and other good shit than the pearled variety, which has that stuff polished off. Pearled barley is super creamy and easier to find in most stores, so just use what you've got. For hulled barley, cook 1 cup of the grain in 3 cups of water in a saucepan with a pinch of salt. Bring to a boil, then cover and simmer that shit until it's tender, 40 to 50 minutes. For pearled, keep the grain-to-water ration the same, but simmer it uncovered until it's tender, about 25 minutes. Want it less creamy? Just rinse that shit when it's done cooking.

COUSCOUS

Couscous cooks quickly since technically it's a pasta, not a grain. Don't believe us? Look that shit up. These mini motherfuckers will be ready in 10 minutes flat. Throw 1 cup couscous into a pot or bowl with a lid and a pinch of salt. Add 1¼ cups boiling water, stir, and throw that lid on. No heat under the pot or nothing. Just let that sit for 8 minutes, then fluff the couscous with a fork and serve. Fucking done.

MILLET

Yeah, millet kinda looks like birdseed, but it's cheap as fuck and deserves more love in the kitchen. It's like a cross between quinoa and brown rice and worthy of a test run on your plate. Throw 1 cup of millet in a medium pot over medium heat and sauté it around until it smells toasty, about 2 minutes. Add 2 cups water and a pinch of salt and simmer that shit, covered, until the millet is tender, 25 to 35 minutes.

QUINOA

Some people cook this protein-packed grain like rice but treat it like pasta. To cook, bring 2 cups water to boil in a medium pot with a pinch of salt, drop in ½ cup quinoa and simmer, uncovered, until the quinoa is tender, 15 to 20 minutes. Drain away any water that's left.

BROWN RICE

You might think this is some hippie health food, but it packs way more health benefits and flavor than white rice. We've always got a big pot of cooked brown rice in the fridge, and your ass should, too. Shit, you could even freeze it into whatever portions you like and heat it up as you need it. If you're still giving this motherfucker the side-eye, try out the short-grain variety (below). That nutty, delicious son of a bitch will make you forget white rice altogether. You can cook the long-grain variety in the same way, but that shit is gonna take about 15 minutes longer and an extra ½ cup water.

>> Make about 4 cups

1 teaspoon olive or coconut oil (optional)*

2 cups short-grain brown rice

Pinch of salt

3½ cups water

BASIC POT OF BROWN RICE

1 In a medium saucepan, heat the oil (if using) over medium heat. Add the rice and sauté that shit until it smells a little nutty, about 2 minutes. Add the salt and water and stir. Bring to a simmer, then reduce the heat, cover, and let this very softly simmer until all the water is absorbed and the rice is tender, about 35 minutes.

2 Did you fuck up the heat and the rice is tender but there's still water? Just drain that shit. Is the rice not done but all the water is gone? Just stir in more a little more water, turn the heat down, and keep going. Don't let some tiny-ass rice get you off your game. YOU. GOT. THIS.

* This oil business is optional but it gives the rice a nuttier taste. Your call, champ.

* HOW TO MELT CHOCOLATE

There's lots of occasions these days where you need to melt some fucking chocolate. Lunch, dinner, during a work call, whenever. To avoid a bowl of grainy mud, follow our instructions and dessert will be right around the fucking corner.

METHOD 1: MICROWAVE

Slowly heat your chocolate in the microwave in 30-second increments and stir after each until it's completely melted. The total length of time will depend on how much chocolate you're fucking with. Don't get crazy and try to do that shit in one big go because it'll get all messed up. We promise, we've been there.

METHOD 2: DOUBLE BOILER

No microwave? No problem. You get to build your own double boiler like a motherfucking boss. Grab a medium saucepan and fill it with 2 to 3 inches of water. Throw an all-metal bowl on top of that and be sure the whole mouth of the pan is covered and that the water inside isn't touching the bottom of the metal bowl. Put this over medium-low heat and add the chocolate to the bowl. The steam will melt the chocolate, just keep stirring and trust the fucking method. When the chocolate looks all smooth, remove from the heat and take the bowl off the pan. Obviously the bowl is gonna be hot as hell, so be careful—otherwise you're good.

WTF IS THAT?

Throughout the book, you may have encountered some ingredients that had you scratching your head and asking "What the fuck?" Here are some answers.

BRAGG LIQUID AMINOS

Yeah, more hippie shit. It tastes and looks a lot like soy sauce but has a little something extra that's hard to explain. It's fucking delicious though, and totally something you should keep in hand. You can find this sauce near the soy sauce or vinegars at most stores or, again, on the goddamn Internet.

LIQUID SMOKE

This shit does exactly what you think it does: adds a smoky flavor to whateverthefuck you are cooking up. It is made by collecting the smoke from burning wood chips, letting that cool, and adding a little water to the mix. It adds a shit-ton of flavor but is easy to overdo, so go easy when you're measuring that shit out. Sure you can do this yourself if you are crazy about that DIY shit, but we recommend you just buy a bottle and save yourself the work. It's near the BBQ sauce at the store, so stop thinking you can't find it. It's there.

MAGGI SEASONING

This is like amped-up soy sauce made from fermented wheat protein but tastes FUCKING AMAZING. It's like a super-rich umami punch with a little bit of herbiness. Originally developed in Switzerland, it's now an obsession all over the world and in our kitchen. It's cheap and widely available online, in a variety of Asian markets, and near the soy sauce in many grocery stores. But if for some reason you just can't find it, use soy sauce in its place.

MASA HARINA

Masa harina is made from corn that has been dried, treated in a solution of lime and water, and then ground into a dough. This fresh masa is then dried and powdered to become shelf-stable masa harina. You can find it near the other flours in the market or by the canned salsas. Don't try subbing in corn flour or corn meal because they aren't treated with lime and they just won't fucking work for any recipe that calls specifically for masa harina. Just wait until you have the real thing.

NOOCH

Nutritional yeast, or nooch if you're cool like that, is some real throwback hippie shit. Sold in flake form, it's deactivated yeast and makes everything taste kinda cheesy. It's packed with B_{12}, folate, selenium, zinc, and protein. You can find it in bulk bins at some grocery stores, in jars near the soy sauce sometimes, and on the Internet. It is not the same thing as brewer's yeast, which you don't ever fucking need.

PANKO BREAD CRUMBS

There are regular bread crumbs and then there are panko bread crumbs, their more glamorous older sister. Panko is much lighter than traditional bread crumbs and are large, coarse flakes rather than tiny-ass sand-looking pieces. The crumbs are used to coat all types of fried and baked shit because they stay crispier longer than regular bread crumbs. You can grab a box of these fuckers somewhere near the soy sauce in your grocery store or near the rest of the bread crumbs.

TEMPEH

This shit is fucking delicious but doesn't sound that way outta the gate, we get it. It's a brick made of fermented soybeans, and because it is fermented, it sometimes might look like it has some mold on it, but just fucking go with it. It adds a great texture and a kinda nutty taste to whateverthefuck you are cooking. One cup of tempeh has 30 goddamn grams of protein in it, so you have no excuses to not try it. You can find it in the fridge of a well-stocked grocery store and the Internet.

TOFU

Everybody knows what this is, but most people have no fucking clue how it's made or how to fucking cook it. Tofu is made from soy milk that has been curdled and then drained of the liquid. The remaining solid stuff is molded into bricks. Served alone it can be soft and have no fucking flavor, so think of it more as something that needs to be fucking seasoned rather than as an ingredient that's bringing any flavor to the table. One cup of tofu has 20 grams of protein, is rich in calcium and iron, and is cholesterol-free, so stop being afraid and try this fucker out at home. You can find it in the fridge section packed in water and in aseptic containers near the soy sauce at the store.

PANTRY STAPLES

Here we piled together a list of simple shit you need to be able to cook like the true boss you are. We know it looks kinda long, but trust us, you'll use all of it if you're cooking like you should. This is basic grocery store shit, so you shouldn't have to change up your shopping routine to find any of this stuff. Now make a list, get your ass to the store, and be nice as fuck to the cashier. They could probably use it. Unless you've bagged groceries to pay bills, you don't know the struggle.

BASIC DRIED HERBS AND SPICES

» One good, all-purpose, no-salt seasoning blend
» Basil
» Black pepper
» Cayenne pepper
» Celery seed
» Chili powder
» Cinnamon
» Cumin
» Curry powder, no-salt
» Garlic powder (granulated garlic is cool, too)
» Onion powder
» Oregano
» Salt
» Smoked paprika
» Thyme

PANTRY SHIT

» Olive oil (we use extra virgin olive oil everywhere it says olive oil in here because we love that shit)
» A neutral-tasting oil: peanut, safflower, or grapeseed
» Soy sauce or tamari
» A nut butter you prefer: peanut, almond, tahini, whatever
» Rice vinegar
» One other vinegar you prefer: apple cider, balsamic, white wine, whateverthefuck you find
» Your favorite grain (short-grain brown rice for the motherfucking win)
» Your favorite pasta noodles

» Canned low-sodium diced tomatoes
» Your favorite dried and canned beans. (Keep both stocked for when you can take your time and when you're in a hurry.)
» Your go-to flour: whole wheat pastry, all-purpose, rice, whatever your favorite shit is

VEGETABLE BASICS

» Yellow onions
» Garlic bulbs
» Carrots
» Some kind of leafy green, such as cabbage, spinach, or kale
» Frozen green peas or edamame

If you're able to keep most of this at your place, you should always be able to make something to eat even if the fridge looks bare. Don't stress if you can't get this all at once because money is tight or whatever. It takes time to get your cabinet game on lock, so be patient with yourself and keep a running list of what you need on your cell phone. That will: (1) keep you from buying six things of cinnamon in two months (we've been there); and (2) help you make sure you're grabbing exactly what you need when shit goes on sale.

FAT RUNDOWN

When it comes to cooking and baking, not all oils are created equal or work for every job. Here's a quick rundown on what to use and where to use it. No matter what you pick, heat your oils up until they shimmer then you can get to cooking. Smoking means your shit is too hot, so turn it down or use another oil because you already fucked it up.

AVOID

Right out of the gate, DO NOT go buying some bullshit like these:

» Vegetable oil

» Any partially hydrogenated oils

» Canola oil

Most of these oils are highly refined and offer no nutritional trade-off. Grab something else and get your money's worth.

LOW- TO MEDIUM-HEAT OILS:

» Olive oil

» Unrefined/virgin coconut oil (this one tastes like coconut, stable at room temp)

» Any of the high-heat oils listed at right

HIGH-HEAT OILS:

» Refined coconut oil (no coconut taste, stable at room temp)

» Peanut oil

» Safflower oil

» Grapeseed oil

OILS FOR DRIZZLING, DRESSINGS, AND EXTRA FLAVOR

» Extra virgin olive oil

» Toasted sesame oil

» Avocado oil

HOW TO MAKE PESTO

Pesto is just a sauce you make by pounding up herbs and nuts, so get the fuck out of your basic basil bullshit. Sure, that's an OG classic, but you've gotta branch out. You can use cilantro, parsley, spinach, kale, or a little bit of everything together and that shit is still a pesto. Try changing out the almonds for walnuts, pine nuts, peanuts, what the fuck ever. We've given you the classic basil pesto, cilantro, greens, and sun-dried tomato recipes, but feel free to substitute your ass off with any of these ingredients. Not sure where to use your new pesto skills? Toss it with some noodles, rice, roasted veggies, or use as a new favorite potato salad dressing. Swirl these fuckers into your favorites soup, replace mayo with pesto in your favorite sammie or wrap, spread it on pizza dough, or use a tablespoon or two as the base to a salad dressing. Fucking endless options. Can't use it all? Freeze it for later.

» **Makes about 1¼ cups**

2½ cups packed torn basil leaves, cilantro or whatever herb/ green combo you're going for

⅔ cup slivered or sliced almonds or pine nuts, toasted (see page 46)

2 garlic cloves, roughly chopped

¼ cup olive oil

¼ cup water

1 teaspoon grated lemon zest

2 tablespoons fresh lemon juice

2 tablespoon nutritional yeast (nooch)*

½ teaspoon salt

BASIC HERB PESTO

In a food processor, combine all the ingredients and blend until smooth-ish. No food processor? Calm the fuck down. Just put the nuts in a plastic bag and smash them until they're tiny and chop the garlic and basil up super small, too. Mix all of it together with a fork until it looks like a paste.

WTF? See page 181.

Wanna mix it up? Sub out the almonds for roasted peanuts and use lime juice. Toss that shit with some rice noodles, sliced peppers, carrots, and cucumbers for a fucking delicious cold noodle salad.

SUN-DRIED TOMATO PESTO

COOK TIME 5 MIN

>> Makes about 2 cups

Throw the sun-dried tomatoes, nuts, garlic, basil, chiles, salt, and nooch into a food processor. Pulse that shit until the tomatoes start getting broken up, then drizzle in the lemon juice and oil, still pulsing the food processor, until a coarse pesto starts to form. This does not need to be smooth at all, just make sure there are no big chunks. This will keep in the fridge for at least 1 week, so you can throw it over hot pasta, spread it on sammies, or use it in our Summer Tomato Tart (page 139).

* About two 8-ounce jars.

** WTF? See page 181.

1½ cups oil-packed sun-dried tomatoes,* with some of the oil in there, too, no stress

⅔ cup slivered or sliced almonds or pine nuts, toasted (see page 46)

4 garlic cloves, roughly chopped

¼ cup chopped fresh basil

1 to 2 small fresh red chiles, such as Fresnos, chopped

½ teaspoon salt

2 tablespoons nutritional yeast (nooch)**

2 tablespoons fresh lemon juice

¼ cup olive oil

WILTED GREENS PESTO

>> Makes about 1¼ cups

2 cups torn greens, such as spinach, kale, arugula, or whatever is wilting and dying in your fridge

1 cup chopped fresh herbs, such as cilantro, dill, basil, parsley, or a mix

1 cup slivered or sliced almonds or walnuts, toasted (see page 46)

2 garlic cloves, roughly chopped

⅓ cup olive oil

¼ cup water

1 teaspoon grated lemon zest

3 tablespoons fresh lemon juice

½ teaspoon salt

In a food processor, combine all the ingredients and blend until smooth-ish. No food processor? Calm the fuck down. Just put the nuts in a plastic bag and smash them until they're tiny and chop the rest of that shit up super small, too. Mix all of it together with a fork until it looks like a paste.

Be warned: After we nailed this recipe down we started adding these fuckers to everything. They improve almost everything, like our Romaine Hearts Salad with Horseradish and Dill Dressing (page 56), and they can even improve your fucking attitude. Put a couple on the nightstand before you go to bed, start your morning with a crouton or two. Have you tried it? Okay then, don't knock it.

HOMEMADE OLD BAY CROUTONS

COOK TIME 30 MIN

》Makes enough for many salads

½ loaf day-old sourdough bread

3 tablespoons olive oil

2 tablespoons fresh lemon juice

2 tablespoons red wine vinegar

2 tablespoons Old Bay seasoning

2 teaspoons garlic powder

1 Crank the oven to 400°F.

2 Cut up the bread into bite-size pieces. You should get around 5 cups. In a big bowl, combine the oil, lemon juice, vinegar, Old Bay, and garlic powder. Add the bread pieces and mix that fucker up to make sure all the pieces get some love.

3 Pour the mixture onto a baking sheet, spread out, and bake for 20 minutes, stirring it halfway through to make sure that shit don't burn. Serve right away or store them in an airtight container.

COOK TIME 10 MIN

》Make I double pie crust

2½ cups all-purpose flour

2 tablespoons cane sugar

½ teaspoon salt

1 stick nondairy butter, frozen for at least an hour and chopped into chunks

4 tablespoons coconut oil or shortening, chopped into chunks and frozen for at least an hour

½ cup ice-cold water

This is our favorite extra-flaky pie crust for when you really wanna flex. This makes one double crust, so if you only need a bottom crust, just halve the recipe. But a smart motherfucker would make it as is, wrap that extra crust in some plastic wrap, and stick that shit in the freezer for a rainy day. Just let it thaw for a bit on the counter before rolling it out.

FLAKY PIE CRUST

1 In a medium mixing bowl, stir together the flour, cane sugar, and salt.

2 Dump the chopped-up cold butter and coconut oil into the flour bowl. Using a pastry cutter or 2 big-ass forks, mush all the fat into the flour until there aren't any big chunks. It should look like clumpy sand with a bunch of pea-sized fat pebbles in it. If any of the fat starts getting too melted, stick that entire fucking bowl back in the freezer for a few minutes so they can firm up. When you bake up the pie crust those little fat pebbles are gonna melt, leaving little pockets in the crust and making it all flaky. That's why you wanna keep all this as cold as possible.

3 Sprinkle the flour with half of the ice water and stir until a shaggy starts dough to come together. You want it to come together into a ball with as little water as possible because that can make it tough. Add as much of the rest of the water you need to make that shit happen. Pat it together into a ball and cut that shit into two roughly equal parts then kinda pat them into sorta flat disks about the size of a softball. Wrap them each in plastic wrap or throw them in a ziplock bag and keep them cold until you're ready for them.

Life's always better with whipped cream. Here's
our staple recipe we've been using for years. It
never fails.

COCONUT MILK WHIPPED CREAM

COOK TIME 7 MIN

>> **Make about 1½ cups**

1 can (14 ounces) full-fat coconut milk, refrigerated*

2 tablespoons powdered sugar

½ teaspoon vanilla extract (optional)

1 You need some electric beaters or a stand mixer to do this. It doesn't matter how much you lift bro, you're not strong enough to do this by hand. Trust us. Stick a bowl and the beaters in the freezer for 15 minutes to let that shit get frosty.

2 Grab the milk from the fridge without shaking it up. Open up the can and scoop out all the thick white cream on the top half of the can and put it in the chilled bowl. (Leave that clearish liquid in the can and use it for a smoothie or something later. You're welcome.) Sift in the powdered sugar so there aren't any chunks, then add the vanilla (if using).

3 Beat on medium-high until it starts looking all fluffy and whipped cream like, 1 to 2 minutes. Serve right away.

* Put that in the fridge the night before so you know it's cold enough. You could do it 1 hour before you make this, but you're probably gonna forget.

COOK TIME 45 MIN

» **Makes about 2 cups**

3 cups (about 1 pound) blueberries*

1 cup cane sugar

Pinch of salt

¼ cup fresh lemon juice (1 to 2 lemons)

2 sprigs of fresh thyme**

You'll need this recipe as part of the Blueberry-Thyme Marble Rolls (page 27), but you can also just make this shit and keep it in your fridge. Goes great on just about anything breakfast-ish. And it's versatile: You can sub out the fruit. The herb. It's a literal dump-and-stir, but people will be impressed you made your own preserves. Low-key food flex. You're welcome.

BLUEBERRY-THYME PRESERVES

Grab your largest saucepan and throw the blueberries, sugar, and salt in there. Set it over medium-high heat, stir it around, and kinda smash the berries as you go. At first you're gonna be like "This shit is dry as hell and isn't gonna work," but you're wrong. Sit tight and watch how much fucking liquid starts appearing as the berries and sugar break down. Once you've got something of a simmer goin', turn the temperature down to medium heat and stir in the lemon juice and thyme sprigs. Easy. Now just stir it to keep the preserves from sticking to the pan until the berry mixture is thick, and you know, looks like jam, 30 to 40 minutes. Remove from the heat and pull out those now-fucked-up-looking little thyme sprigs. Let the preserves cool for a couple minutes before putting them in a jar and sticking them in the fridge. This will keep in the fridge for at least 2 weeks.

*This recipe is flexible as hell, so feel free to replace blueberries with another berry like strawberries, blackberries, cherries, or a mix. Just take out the thyme since it doesn't go with everything. And you can use frozen, too. They'll just take a little longer to thicken up when you cook this shit.

**Optional but awesome. If you're using a different fruit you might leave this out or sub in rosemary, lemon verbena, or something else you got lying around. Just taste the berry and the herb together to make sure it makes sense.

Passion fruit, or lilikoi, is a tropical fruit that's so damn good we can't stop eating it. It's solid spread on toast, stirred into iced tea, drizzled over yogurt or vanilla ice cream, and mixed into our Passion Fruit Cheesecake (page 151). If you can't find fresh passion fruit where you live, check the freezer section. Then just defrost and then follow the recipe like normal. You won't ever want to go a day without some of this in your fridge. Trust us.

PASSION FRUIT PRESERVES

》 Makes one 8-ounce jar's worth

2 cups passion fruit pulp with seeds

1 to 1½ cups cane sugar, depending on how sweet you like shit

¼ cup lemon juice

1 Pour everything together in a small saucepan and simmer for 30 minutes, stirring every few minutes, until the preserves start to thicken up. About 15 minutes into all this you'll notice all the flesh around the seeds kinda melt off. At that point if you wanna skim out some of the seeds, go for it. We like to keep about one-third of them in there because their texture is nice and they make the finished preserves look classy as fuck.

2 An easy test to know if the preserves are ready: Stick a spoon in the freezer for a few minutes. When it's nice and cold, drop some preserves on the back and then run your finger through the preserves. If the preserves stay put and don't bleed into the empty space left by your finger, you're good to go.

3 Store in an airtight container in the fridge and it should last in there at least a month.

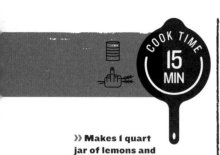

COOK TIME
15 MIN

» **Makes 1 quart jar of lemons and accompanying goodness**

1 quart glass jar with lid

9 lemons, washed (about 1½ pounds)

½ cup salt

This is an old-school way of making citrus last, and it remains one of the very best ways. Chop up some of the lemons and add them to pasta, blend them into sauces, and toss them with some veggies. You can take as little as you need out of the jar at a time so you'll always have some laying around. Need more guidance? Try our Preserved Lemon Vinaigrette (page 210). And, yeah, you can do this recipe with limes too.

PRESERVED LEMONS

1 This recipe isn't super exact so don't worry too much about getting all the measurements right. It's more about the technique and time. OK, here we go. Cut off the little nubby end on both sides of the lemons, then cut them into four sections from the end like you were cutting a cake. Don't cut all the way to the bottom, though; you still want the slices attached to each other by at least ½ inch of uncut citrus. This is the hardest part of the recipe and it's not even fucking hard. Leave 1 lemon uncut.

2 Sprinkle 1 tablespoon of salt into the bottom of the jar. Put around 1 tablespoon of salt inside each lemon, in the cut-up parts, and kinda rub it around to pack it in. Place the lemon into the jar. Keep doing this shit and pack the lemons in the jar as tight as you can. Sure, some are gonna spill open and some might even rip a little, but it's cool. Just do your best.

3 When the jar is all packed with lemon, squeeze the juice of the remaining lemon over the top and pack down the lemons again, trying to get out any of the air bubbles. Put on the lid and let this all sit overnight. The next day sometime check on the lemons and push them down again and get out any remaining air bubbles. They should have released more juice by now so this should be easier. Make sure that there's enough juice in there to cover all the lemons so that they can pickle in peace.

4 Place jar in a cool spot like your pantry. Check on them every couple of days for 2 weeks, making sure that all the lemons stay underneath the juice. It takes 15 seconds. Easy.

5 After 2 weeks, the rinds will be soft and you can stick the jar in the refrigerator and stop babysitting it. They will keep at least 6 months.

RED ONIONS

BRUSSELS

DILL PICKLES

KUMQUATS

These tangy sons of bitches add a crunch to any salad or sandwich, or try 'em in a taco or in a rando rice bowl. Plus the pink makes even the most basic dishes look elevated as hell. They are the perfect way to make even the saddest meal look and taste way fucking better. Keep a jar of these in your fridge at all times and send your fan mail directly to us.

QUICK-PICKLED RED ONIONS

》Makes 1 packed 12-ounce jar

½ cup rice vinegar

½ cup apple cider vinegar

½ cup water

1 teaspoon salt

Pinch of cane sugar

1 large red onion, thinly sliced into rings

1 In a small saucepan, combine both vinegars, the water, salt, and sugar and bring to a boil.

2 Stack all the sliced onions in a 12-ounce glass jar, one that's okay to take some heat and has a lid. Once the vinegar is simmering, remove from the heat and pour it over the onions, making sure they're all covered. Let it cool on the counter for a couple minutes then toss on the lid and stick it in the fridge.

3 Serve after 30 minutes or let them hang out in there until they're all the way chilled. Eat within 2 weeks.

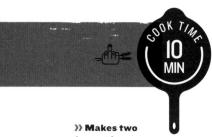

**» Makes two
1-quart jars**

2 pounds Kirby
or other pickling
cucumbers,*
quartered lengthwise

10 large sprigs of dill

2 cups water

1 cup white vinegar

2 tablespoons salt

2 teaspoons sugar

1 teaspoon black
peppercorns

1 teaspoon celery
seeds

*Don't know shit about
cucumbers? Read up on
page 229.*

Stop spending your hard-earned money on motherfuckin' pickles. This is cheaper and will taste better because YOU made them. See how buying this book has already saved you money? This cookbook is practically paying for itself. You're gonna need two 1-quart glass jars with tight-fitting lids. Got 'em? Okay.

REFRIGERATOR DILL PICKLES

1 Divide the quartered cucumbers and dill between two 1-quart glass jars. You know how pickle jars should look.

2 In a saucepan, bring the water, vinegar, salt, sugar, peppercorns, and celery seeds to a boil over medium-high heat. Keep stirring that shit to dissolve the salt and sugar, a minute or two. And yeah, it's gonna make your place smell like vinegar, but that's pickle life for ya. Once everything is all dissolved, remove from the heat. Pour that hot brine into the jars, dividing evenly, and then slap on those lids. Let them cool on the counter until they're not crazy hot anymore, about 15 minutes, then stick them in the fridge to chill.

3 These guys are best about 2 days after you make them, and they'll keep for about 2 months in the fridge.

Ever notice how we all just universally respect anyone who makes their own sauce? Here's a basic recipe that you can build on to make it your own. If you don't have a sauce specialist in your life, you can fill that void. You can be that person. First you get the tomatoes, then you get the power.

HOUSE MARINARA

1 Grab a medium stockpot. Chop up the onion. Dice up the carrot into pieces about the size of a pea. Mince the garlic up small. You can do this shit in your sleep.

2 Warm the oil in the stockpot over medium heat. Add the onion and sauté it until begins to look golden in some places, 4 to 5 minutes. Add the carrot and cook for another 2 minutes. Add the garlic, thyme, and red pepper flakes. This should be smelling fucking choice right now. Grab the whole tomatoes, and smash them in your hands into a bunch of pieces and stir them into the pot as you go. Keep doing this until all the tomatoes are smashed up, and add ¾ of a cup of the juice from the can to the pot. Turn down the heat to medium-low and simmer this uncovered for about 20 minutes until all the tomatoes are broken down. Taste and add more garlic, thyme, salt, or whateverthefuck you think it needs.

3 If you like a smoother sauce, throw that shit in the blender or use a stick blender to get rid of some of the chunks. This sauce will keep in the fridge for a week.

* Or you could use 5 cloves of roasted garlic (page 235) to mix it up.

COOK TIME 35 MIN

》Make about 4 cups of sauce

Half a large onion, white or yellow

1 carrot

3 garlic cloves*

1 teaspoon olive oil

1 (28-ounce) can of whole tomatoes

1 teaspoons dried thyme

Pinch of red pepper flakes

Salt

COOK TIME 120 MIN

» **Makes enough for 4 individual pizzas**

4 cups all-purpose or whole wheat pastry flour or a mix of the two flours, plus more for rolling out

½ teaspoon salt

1¾ cups warm water*

2¼ teaspoons dry yeast**

1 teaspoon sugar

2 tablespoons olive oil

This is our fav, dummy-proof recipe for perfect homemade pizza. Read the recipe all the way through before you start and you'll have no problems. READ. ALL OF IT. FIRST. DUMMY. Sure, this takes a while, but most of that time you're just fucking around waitin' for this shit to rise.

EVERYDAY PIZZA DOUGH

1 Whisk the flour and salt together in a big bowl and set it aside.

2 In a small glass, mix together the warm water, yeast, and sugar and wait a couple of minutes and see if the glass looks kinda foamy at the top. If nothing fucking happens, then your yeast is old as shit and died so you need to get some new stuff. RIP.

3 When the yeast is ready to go, pour that whole glass into the flour bowl and stir it together until a shaggy dough comes together. Still got a ton of flour hanging out in the bowl? Add a little bit more water, up to ¼ cup more, a tablespoon at time, until there are no more piles of dry flour. This shit depends a lot on how much moisture is in the flour, so it changes all the time. SCIENCE! Knead the dough for a couple minutes until a smooth ball comes together. (WTF is kneading? See page 29.) Rub the olive oil over the dough and put it in a bowl. Cover that shit with a clean kitchen towel and let it rise someplace that isn't too cold or drafty until it's about doubled in size, about 1½ hours.

4 When it's all big and ready to go, punch it down to let some of that gas escape and just knead that shit a couple more times to get it back into a ball shape. At this point you can divide the dough into four equal parts and roll out the dough to make your pizzas, or throw the dough in a zip-top bag and stick it in the fridge for the next week. Just let it warm back up to about room temp before trying to roll it out after it's been in the fridge.

5 To roll out the dough, throw some extra flour out on your counter and pat some on your rolling pin. (No rolling pin? Go fucking get one and stop trying to use a wine bottle. It won't end well, trust us.) Roll your dough out into a circle-ish shape about ¼ inch thick. For baking instructions, see page 104.

* Like the temperature of tea that you could tell used to be warm but has been sitting out for a couple minutes.

** Or one ¼-ounce envelope of yeast.

We don't need to sell you on how great parmesan is on just about everything. But parm without the cheese? It's not only possible but it's so goddamn delicious you won't miss the other stuff. Now before we get a cease-and-desist from big dairy, enjoy this lactose-free parmesan.

PANTRY PARM

Throw everything in a food processor or blender and run that shit until everything is reduced to crumbs. Throw it in an airtight jar and keep it in your fridge for about 3 weeks.

* WTF? See page 181.

COOK TIME
5 MIN

» Makes about 2 cups

1¼ cups sliced almonds

⅔ cup nutritional yeast (nooch)*

2 tablespoons garlic powder

Zest from 1 lemon

1 teaspoon salt

COOK TIME 110 MIN

>> **Makes enough for several pizzas**

MARINADE

¾ cup vegetable broth

¾ cup dry red wine

⅓ cup Bragg Liquid Aminos,* tamari, or soy sauce

4 garlic cloves, minced

2 teaspoons liquid smoke*

1 mounded tablespoon chopped fennel seeds

2 teaspoons onion powder

2 teaspoons smoked paprika

½ teaspoon black pepper

½ teaspoon mustard powder

¼ to ½ teaspoon cayenne pepper, to taste

BEETS

6 small beets, peeled and extremely thinly sliced

2 tablespoons olive oil

WTF? See page 180.

If you trusted us with carrot hot dogs in our second book, *Bad Manners: Party Grub*, then follow us on this pepperoni-flavored beet journey. There's some marinating here, so give yourself enough time. When this shit inevitably becomes a trend and it's everywhere to the annoyingth degree, we will not apologize. Learn all about beets on page 222 so you can answer all the questions.

BEETERONI

1 Make the marinade: In a small saucepan, combine all the marinade ingredients and bring to a simmer over medium heat for about 5 minutes. Then turn off the heat.

2 Meanwhile, place all the sliced beets in a large baking pan. Pour the hot marinade over the beets and cover the pan with foil or whatever you have lying around. Let the beets sit for at least 1 hour and up to overnight.

3 When you are ready to start the damn thing, crank the oven to 400°F. Grease a large baking sheet really well.

4 Drain the marinade from the beets, reserving like ½ cup or so. Toss the drained slices with the olive oil. Place the slices on the greased baking sheet, spreading in a single layer if possible. Bake for 10 minutes and then flip the slices and brush the slices with some of the reserved marinade. Bake until most of beets have started to curl at the edges, another 8 to 10 minutes. You want the beets to look somewhat blackened on both sides and slightly crispy. Remove from the oven when they look well cooked and baste lightly once more with the reserved marinade as they cool.

5 Throw these tasty fuckers on a pizza, on some bread for mind-blowing crostini, or just eat them right off the damn baking sheet.

Add this shit to sautéed greens, fold it into any pasta, or add to the top of a pizza for some protein and extra flavor. You'll make this staple so fucking much that soon you won't even need to look at this recipe. ALL SEASON, ANY REASON, TEMPEH CRUMBLE IS READY TO RUMBLE.

ALL-SEASONS TEMPEH CRUMBLE

COOK TIME
8 MIN

>> **Makes about 1 cup**

Grab a large skillet or wok and warm up the oil over medium heat. Using your hands, crumble in the tempeh into pieces no bigger than a nickel. Smaller is better than big chunks, but there's really no wrong way to do this shit. Add the onion and sauté them together until the tempeh starts to brown, about 5 minutes. Sprinkle in the soy sauce all over the pan, stir, then add the fennel seeds, basil, oregano, and thyme. Sauté for 30 seconds, then fold in the lemon juice and garlic. Remove from the heat and shake in some pepper flakes if you're into that.

* WTF? See page 180.

** Fennel seeds give this that sausage taste without all the meat. You can leave them out if you don't have them but it won't be the same.

2 teaspoons olive oil

1 block (8 ounces) tempeh

1 yellow onion, chopped

1 tablespoon soy sauce or Bragg Liquid Aminos*

2 teaspoons chopped fennel seeds**

1 teaspoon dried basil

1 teaspoon dried oregano

1 teaspoon dried thyme

1 tablespoon fresh lemon juice

3 garlic cloves, minced

Red pepper flakes (optional)

Want it even simpler? Leave out the dried herbs. Wanna make it a side? Add 6 cups chopped chard, kale, or spinach when you add the garlic and keep sautéing until that shit wilts down, about 2 minutes.

COOK TIME 15 MIN

» **Makes enough for 4 sandwiches**

8 ounces tempeh*

1 cup vegetable broth or water

¼ cup soy sauce or tamari

2 tablespoons fresh lemon juice

1 tablespoon pure maple syrup or other syrupy sweetener

1 tablespoon smoked paprika

4 garlic cloves, thickly sliced

2 teaspoons liquid smoke*

1 tablespoon olive oil

WTF? See page 180.

Use these in a sandwich: Our Pear, Tempeh, and Arugula Sandwich (page 100) is def a winner, or you can free-style and do whatever you want. If you need more help with how to assemble a sandwich, check around on the Internet and then go cry yourself to sleep.

SMOKY TEMPEH SLICES

1 Slice the tempeh into planks about ¼ inch thick and 2 inches long. No need to fucking measure it out, just eyeball it.

2 In a saucepan, stir together the broth, soy sauce, lemon juice, maple syrup, paprika, garlic, and liquid smoke and bring to a simmer over medium-low heat. Add the tempeh and gently stir them around. They won't all be covered, just fucking make it work the best you can. Simmer everything together for about 30 seconds.

3 Remove from the heat and pour it all into a shallow dish like a pie pan or some shit. Cover that up and stick it in the fridge to marinate for at least 4 hours and up to 8 hours. Yeah, plan ahead, you lazy fuck.

4 When you're ready to fry up your tempeh, in a large skillet or wok, heat up the oil over medium heat. Lay the tempeh slices down in one layer (reserve the marinade) and cook them until the tempeh starts to brown, 2 to 3 minutes on each side. When it starts to look a little dry in there or the tempeh feels like it might be sticking, just add a couple spoonfuls of the marinade.

5 Once the tempeh is browned on both sides, you are ready to make a badass sandwich.

Sometimes a dish just needs a lil extra flavor and crunch sprinkled just before serving and boy, have we got just the shit for you. This is a dope last-minute addition to any pasta, tray of roasted veggies, or sprinkled directly into your mouth hovering over the kitchen sink at 2 a.m. A tightly sealed jar of this will keep in the fridge for at least two weeks and will save even the lamest of leftovers. Sprinkle responsibly.

PANKO PASTA TOPPING

In a medium skillet, warm the oil over medium-low heat. Add the panko and stir that shit around so everything gets some oil on it. Keep stirring until it starts to look a little golden, 3 to 5 minutes. Don't go crazy, it's at medium-low. Sometimes people just read "HEAT" and fucking crank their stoves. ANYWAY, stir in the lemon zest, garlic powder, paprika, and salt until it's all mixed in. Then remove from the heat and pour the topping onto a plate. Use right away or let it cool before storing. This tasty topping will keep for 2 weeks stored in an airtight container in the fridge.

COOK TIME 10 MIN

》Makes about 1½ cups

3 tablespoons olive oil

1½ cups panko bread crumbs

1 teaspoon grated lemon zest

¼ teaspoon garlic powder

¼ teaspoon paprika

¼ teaspoon salt

>> **Makes about 1 cup**

⅓ cup rice vinegar*

¼ cup olive, grapeseed, or avocado oil

1 tablespoon soy sauce

1 tablespoon pure maple syrup or agave

2 teaspoons toasted sesame oil

2 garlic cloves, grated**

½-inch piece fresh ginger, grated**

This is entry-level shit you should have on hand in the fridge. It's equally effective on salads as it is cold noodle dishes. Plus you sound hella sophisticated sayin' "lemme just whip up a sesame vinaigrette real quick."

SESAME VINAIGRETTE

Whisk everything together in a small glass or shake that fucker up in a screw-top jar. Use within 5 days.

Wanna mix it up? Sub this shit out for our Fresh Chile Vinegar (page 211).

**This isn't as fancy as it sounds. Just grab your Microplane or cheese grater and, using the smallest holes, grate until you've got a fine paste. Easy shit.*

1. Fresh Chile Vinegar
2. Preserved Lemon Vinaigrette
3. Everyday Vinaigrette
4. Hot Chile Oil
5. Sesame Vinaigrette
6. Horseradish and Dill Dressing

》Makes more than 1½ cups

½ cup sliced or slivered almonds

½ cup hot water

¼ cup olive oil

¼ cup cashew butter, tahini, or almond butter

2 tablespoons fresh lemon juice

2 tablespoons champagne vinegar

1 to 2 tablespoons prepared horseradish, store-bought or homemade (page 215)

2 garlic cloves, chopped

1 tablespoon minced fresh dill

Pinch of salt

Serve this over romaine hearts or your favorite lettuce with our Homemade Old Bay Croutons (page 187) and Quick-Pickled Red Onions (page 195), because you know how to live.

HORSERADISH AND DILL DRESSING

Put the almonds in a glass with hot water and let those fuckers soak for about 15 minutes.

1 When the almonds start feeling sorta soft, throw them in a food processor or blender with half of the water they soaked in. Add the olive oil, cashew butter, lemon juice, vinegar, horseradish, and garlic. Blend it all up until there are no more large almond pieces and it starts to look kinda creamy. You know what the fuck dressing should look like, come on.

2 Add the dill and salt and run it again for another 5 seconds just so it gets chopped up. Chill until you are ready to eat.

Keep a bottle of this in your fridge ready to go and you can whip up a salad in minutes any fucking night of the week. It'll separate while you store it in the fridge. so just shake that shit real good before you use it. It will keep for a week or two, no problem. Wanna make it your own? You can switch out the vinegars with what you like to perfect your favorite combo. Balsamic and champagne? Sounds good. White wine and sherry? Fuck yeah. You do you.

EVERYDAY VINAIGRETTE

Pour all this together in a screw-top jar and shake the fuck out of it. Taste and add more of whatever you think it needs. If you want to mix it up even more, add 2 teaspoons of your favorite dried herb or herb blend and shake that shit in.

* You can also sub in 2 cloves minced garlic if that's your style.

** Chill out, it won't taste like mustard. This just brings the whole dressing together. Trust.

》 Makes about 2 cups

¼ cup diced shallot or sweet onion*

1 tablespoon Dijon mustard**

⅓ cup red wine vinegar

⅓ cup rice vinegar

½ cup olive oil

» **Makes about 1½ cups**

1 cup Frank's RedHot sauce*

¼ cup white vinegar

1 teaspoon soy sauce

2 tablespoons nondairy butter or refined coconut oil

½ teaspoon garlic powder

There's absolutely no fucking reason to buy premade buffalo sauce. Ever. Just mail us your money and we'll light it on fire for you. Look at this recipe. Look how fucking simple this is. Now shut the hell up and make this yourself because it's easy and the simpletons who don't know will be so impressed.

BUFFALO SAUCE

Just throw all the ingredients in a saucepot, stir it around so the garlic powder isn't in a clump, and warm over medium heat until it starts to simmer and all the butter is incorporated. Then remove from the heat. Easy as hell. Never buy shit premade. They're tricking you into buyin' shit you don't need.

* This is not some viral marketing shit. It's just the best brand of hot sauce for Buffalo sauce. You can try other vinegar-based hot sauces, but we can't vouch for that shit.

» **Makes about 1¼ cups**

1 preserved lemon,* seeds removed

3 to 4 garlic cloves, peeled

⅓ cup rice vinegar or white wine vinegar

½ cup olive oil

Serve this over simple greens, roasted veggies, or even as the dressing for a pasta salad. All you.

PRESERVED LEMON VINAIGRETTE

Throw the whole lemon, garlic, and vinegar in a blender or food processor and let that shit rip. With it running, slowly stream in the oil to make sure it gets all mixed in there and doesn't immediately separate. Taste, and depending on the preserved lemon, you might need more vinegar, garlic, or even a pinch of sugar to balance it out.

* Learn how to make these on page 192.

Dress cold noodles with this, use it in slaw, in tofu marinades, anywhere you want to sub in some tasty-ass vinegar.

FRESH CHILE VINEGAR

» Makes about 2½ cups

1 In a small saucepan, combine the vinegar, sugar, and salt and simmer over medium-high heat for 5 minutes, making sure all the sugar and salt have dissolved. Yes, simmering vinegar makes your place smell weird, but it's almost over, so calm the fuck down. Remove from the heat and let it chill on the stove for 2 minutes to cool a little.

2 While that's cooling, grab a large glass jar, at least 16 ounces (but use a 24-ounce one if you've got it just to be safe), and throw in the garlic, ginger, chiles, and peppercorns. Pour in the hot vinegar and let this cool to room temperature, then place it in the fridge to keep infusing and shit. Give it a week before you taste it so it can really show you what it's all about. It will keep for about 2 months in the fridge and will get tastier and spicier the longer it sits.

2 cups rice vinegar

1 tablespoon sugar

1 teaspoon salt

3 garlic cloves, peeled

1 small knob fresh ginger, peeled and sliced into 4 rounds

1 cup bird's-eye chiles, Thai chiles, or your favorite fresh little chiles, scrubbed but whole

1 teaspoon black peppercorns

COOK TIME 10 MIN

》 Makes about ½ cup

½ cup neutral oil, such as safflower or grapeseed

1 tablespoon red pepper flakes

Pinch of salt

This is a cheap way to make something that tastes fucking delicious and looks all fancy. Don't like heat? We've got lots of suggestions below on how to customize this shit for your palette.

HOT CHILE OIL

In a small saucepan, heat up the oil over medium heat until it's warm but not so hot it's gonna fry shit, about 2 minutes. Remove from the heat and add the pepper flakes and salt and stir it around. Let this chill for about 5 minutes so it gets all infused. Transfer to a glass jar with a lid and let it cool to room temp before using so you get the most flavor out of it. It will keep for about 1 week.

You can do this shit with all kinds of things. Add a clove of garlic and some rosemary for a whole different thing. Add some Sichuan peppercorns and drizzle this over cold noodles. Add a tablespoon of grated lemon zest and use this shit in salad dressings. Only change: If you're using stuff that isn't all dried out, like garlic and fresh herbs, fish them outta there when the oil has cooled completely so that this shit doesn't spoil too fast.

We hate buying premade shit. We like ingredients, not products. So even though nondairy cheeses have come a long fucking way in the last couple of years they're still expensive as fuck and we'll eat them as soon as they enter our apartment. Thus we had to come up with a cheese sauce that is easy and fast to make using what we already stay stocked up on at home. This tasty son of a bitch is the result and we couldn't be prouder.

CASHEW CHEESE SAUCE

1 In a bowl, soak the cashews in hot water for 15 minutes. Drain the cashews and throw out the nut bath water.

2 Transfer the cashews to a blender, add the rest of the ingredients and blend until smooth. See? This is super fucking easy.

3 Transfer to a medium saucepan and cook over medium heat, stirring until the sauce has thickened up how you want it. Want something looser to drizzle over pizzas? Cook for 4 to 5 minutes. Want something thicker to have on sandwiches? Cook for 6 to 7 minutes. Your cheese, your rules.

WTF? See page 181.

COOK TIME 25 MIN

》 Makes about 1½ cups

1 cup cashews

2 cups vegetable broth

2 tablespoons olive oil

2 tablespoons tapioca flour/starch or all-purpose flour

1 tablespoon nutritional yeast (nooch)*

1 tablespoon fresh lemon juice

1 teaspoon garlic powder

1 teaspoon onion powder

1 teaspoon salt

COOK TIME 8 MIN

» **Makes about 1¼ cups**

2 stalks fresh lemongrass (6 inches long), tough outer layer removed, roughly chopped*

6 garlic cloves

3 to 6 fresh chiles, such as serrano or jalapeno

3 medium shallots or ½ white onion, chopped

2 tablespoons chopped fresh ginger (about 2 inches)

¾ cup chopped fresh cilantro

½ cup fresh basil leaves**

1½ teaspoons grated lime zest (about 3 limes)

1 tablespoon fresh lime juice

1 teaspoon ground coriander***

1 teaspoon ground cumin

1 teaspoon cane sugar or pure maple syrup

1 teaspoon salt

2 tablespoons neutral high-heat oil, such as safflower or peanut

Sure you can buy store-bought, but have some fucking faith in yourself and try this shit at home. You can blend, right? Fucking easy. Obviously this paste is great in our Coconut Green Curry with Avocado (page 137), but you can toss a tablespoon or two of this over roasted vegetables, into plain rice, or straight into your fucking mouth. It's always a hit.

GREEN CURRY PASTE

1 Throw everything into a food processor and run that shit until a thick paste forms. You might have to stop, scrape down the sides, and run it again a couple times to really get shit going. Still too thick? Add a tablespoon or two of water. Just enough to help out your shitty machine.

2 Store the paste in an airtight container in the refrigerator for up to 1 week or freeze that shit for easy use in an old ice cube tray and it will keep for 4 to 5 months.

WTF? See page 240

** There's a bunch of different kinds of basil in this world (see page 237). Thai basil works best here because it has a stronger taste than the sweeter Genovese basil you find all over. But use whatever you can find. Any curry is better than no curry at all.

*** Don't have it/don't want to fill up your spice cabinet anymore? Sub in an extra ½ teaspoon cumin and call it a fucking day.

Fresh horseradish looks like an ugly-ass branch stuck near the lettuces at the grocery store. But if you just kinda scratch the skin with your nail and smell, oh shit, you'll know it's horseradish. Store-bought horseradish sauce is legit, but it's worth making it yourself if you ever get the chance to see what the real deal is all about. When you sub this shit in for store-bought horseradish in a recipe, start a little at a time 'cause this is a lot stronger than that simple shit from the store. Use it in our Horseradish and Dill Dressing (page 208), fold a little into mashed potatoes, or just drizzle it on everything like a fucking maniac.

COOK TIME 20 MIN

》 Makes about 1 cup

6-inch piece horseradish root, peeled and chopped (about 1 cup)

½ cup white vinegar

½ teaspoon salt

HOMEMADE HORSERADISH

1 First, this shit is spicy and when you start cutting the horseradish it might hurt your eyes like onions do, so crack a window, throw on some glasses, do what you need to do.

2 Throw the chopped root, vinegar, and salt in a food processor and let that shit run until it's smooth. Add a tablespoon or two of water if you need more liquid in there to get the processor going. Done.

3 Store this in the fridge in a glass container with a tight lid and it'll keep for at least 3 weeks to a month.

GARDEN OF EATIN

Here in the back garden you'll find a guide to all the produce you need to know. We've listed our favorites in alphabetical order for quick refence, with tips on when to buy, how to store them, and why food is always the best medicine. Now read up so you're ready to harvest some health on your next grocery run.

ARTICHOKE

Artichokes look like the kind of vegetable people started eating on a dare. These barbed thistles are related to sunflowers and the plants they grow on can get taller than 6 feet. So obviously eating and preparing these guys is some work, but we wouldn't be into it if they weren't so fucking delicious. Plus they are full of all kinds of phytonutrients like cynarine, which increases bile production in your liver and helps rid your body of cholesterol. They also serve up all the hit minerals like magnesium, manganese, copper, potassium, and phosphorus.

We've got all kinds of cooking tips on page 219, but when you get them home from the store, carve a thin slice off the stem. Sprinkle the leaves with a tiny bit of water and place them in an airtight container. This will last you up to a week, but just cook them as soon as you can. Why fucking wait? Artichokes are in season from late summer to early winter unless you live in California. California supplies almost 100 percent of the country's artichokes so we've always got some of these spiky sons of bitches lying around.

Canned artichokes are a different beast from their fresh brethren but damn tasty nonetheless. You can find them canned, packed in water, and in glass jars, packed in oil. Whatever you choose, they'll be by the olives in the grocery store. We like to chop them up and throw them in salads, especially when we are out of avocado, blend them to add creaminess to dips and sauces, and fold them into pastas to add something interesting. They are easy as fuck just to keep in the pantry for a day when you are out of everything else but still wanna feel a little fancy.

ARUGULA

Rocket, better known as arugula here in the U.S., is a green worth knowing. Its texture is similar to spinach, but it has a sorta peppery taste which is so fucking good on sandwiches, pizza, in pasta, or just in your damn mouth. You hardly have to do anything to it. Throw some lemon juice and olive oil on it with a pinch of salt and that fucker tastes like a billion bucks. It's in the plant family Brassicaceae along with kale, radishes, and cauliflower, which means this guy is hearty as fuck. It grows all year and is resistant to cold weather. Aside from just tasting good, arugula is an excellent source of fiber, folate, calcium, iron, magnesium, phosphorus, potassium, manganese, and vitamins A, C, and K. Eat your fucking vitamins.

Like any green, you want to keep this shit cool and dry when you get it home. Throw it in your fridge in a breathable bag with something in there to help wick away any excess moisture, like a paper towel. This will keep the arugula looking good for at least 4 or 5 days. If you don't use it all in one go, make sure to kinda fluff that shit around so it doesn't settle into a wet ball of leaves and go bad way faster than it should. You wanna get your money's worth. Arugula on its last leg? Make a pesto with it and throw that shit in the freezer for a rainy day. Follow our Basic Herb Pesto recipe on page 184, but sub in arugula and you won't have to throw any scraps away.

DISARM YOUR DINNER

HOW TO COOK FRESH ARTICHOKES

We know artichokes look alien as fuck, but they're really easy to clean up and fucking delicious to eat. You're going to have to put in some work because they've got some barbs and shit you don't want to eat.

Remove the tough outer leaves around the base and cut off the top of the choke, about 1½ inches down. Using scissors, cut the top off any leaves that still have the barb on them. If your artichoke still has its stalk, peel the outside with a vegetable peeler, and do a fresh cut on the bottom.

Now you've got to get the flesh on the leaves and the heart tender so you can eat this fucker up. You can boil them, braise, or parcook and then grill or broil them. When you get to the heart (the bottom of the artichoke where all the leaves connect) use a spoon and scoop out all the hairy guts that sit on top. You don't wanna eat that part, but you def wanna eat the heart.

TO BOIL: Fill a large soup pot with water and put it over high heat. Squeeze the juice of half a lemon into the pot and slice up the other half of the lemon and add it to the water with a big pinch of salt and 2 cloves of smashed garlic. Let the water come to a boil and add the prepped, whole artichokes. Bring to a simmer, cover, and let that shit go for 20 to 40 minutes depending on the size of your artichokes. Stir them around every now and then to make sure every side gets enough time in the water. You can tell they're done when one of the inside leaves can be pulled out without a fucking fight. Pull them out of the water with tongs and set them in a colander. Let them drain for a bit and serve warm with a dipping sauce.

TO GRILL: Cut the prepped artichoke in half lengthwise (through the stem). If you haven't already, scoop out all the hairy guts with a spoon, but don't take out any of the heart, there's a lotta flavor in that motherfucker. Grab a soup pot and follow the directions above for boiling, but start checking on the artichokes after 15 minutes since they'll cook faster when cut in half. Let them drain over the sink for a few minutes while you get the grill going.

Bring your grill to a medium-high heat. In a small bowl, mix together ¼ cup high-heat oil (such as safflower), 2 minced garlic cloves, a pinch of salt, and 2 tablespoons lemon juice.

When the grill is ready to go, brush some of that oil mixture all over the drained artichokes. Throw those thistly bastards on the grill, cut side down, and cook until they get some good grill marks on them but the leaves aren't burnt to shit, 2 to 3 minutes. Flip them over and do the same on the other side. Brush with more of the oil mix if you think it needs it. Serve warm or at room temp with a dip of your choice or just as is.

TO BRAISE: See Wine-Braised Artichokes with Fresh Herbs (page 70).

AVOCADO

Yeah, they are fucking bomb on toast, but avocados don't need to be a guilty brunch pleasure. These fruits (yeah that's right) are legit good for you. Sure they're high in fat, but that's kinda their whole magic. The monounsaturated and polyunsaturated fats in avocados are referred to as "good fats" by all the people in the know. Avocado consumption has been linked to lower levels of bad (LDL) cholesterol, which lord knows we all need. Plus they have about 1 gram of fiber per tablespoon, with around 10 grams in an entire fruit, which is another big-ass plus. Fiber with fat helps you feel full longer, which means no more crazy 2 p.m. candy bar run if you eat right. In fact, a 2013 study found that overweight adults who added half a fresh avocado to their lunch were less likely to feel hungry after eating, which is all any of us really wants, right?

Avocados also help your body better absorb fat-soluble nutrients like vitamins A, D, E, and K, which it is just packed full of.

You want to buy your avocados when they have just a little give to them but aren't mushy or rock-hard and give them a day or two to get the perfect amount of soft. Store them on your countertop, but throw them in the fridge if they get ripe and you aren't gonna use them that day. However you use them—on sandwiches, as a dip, to replace mayo, in salads, whatever—squeeze some citrus juice on the cut-up flesh to keep it from getting brown and fucking gross-looking.

BANANAS

There are more than 1,000 different types of bananas in the world, but chances are you've only ever had the classic grocery store banana: Cavendish. This variety accounts for 47 percent of the bananas grown worldwide and 99 percent of all bananas sold commercially for export all over the globe. And if you think it's the most dominant banana because it's the tastiest, you're dead fucking wrong. It is the easiest to transport long distances and it's resistant to many forms of fungus that take out other bananas. It's def not the sweetest but this is where we are at. And even worse? You've basically been eating the exact same banana your whole life because the Cavendish plant is sterile, which is why you've never eaten a banana seed. So every banana you've ever had is a clone piece cut off another plant made to grow on its own, and thus are genetically identical. Creepy, right?

That spooky shit aside, bananas are an excellent source of vitamin B_6, some vitamin C, and, of course, potassium. Potassium is one of the most important electrolytes in the body, helping to regulate heart function and fluid balance, which is key in regulating blood pressure. Bananas are also soothing to the gastrointestinal tract because of their high content of pectin. This soluble fiber not only lowers cholesterol but also normalizes bowel function. Yeah, that's why people tell you to get these fuckers when you've been sick as shit for a couple of days.

Store your bananas on your countertop and if they get too ripe before you can use them, peel and freeze them to add to smoothies and shakes. They'll last for a couple of months in there and they are clutch in our Banana Date Shake, page 148.

BEANS

We aren't too good to use canned beans. Those fuckers are super handy when you're busy. But nothing, NOTHING, compares to the real shit cooked from scratch.

HOW TO COOK BEANS

Once you got the framework down, throwing together a pot of beans is some of the simplest shit you can do in the kitchen. You just need some goddamn patience. The steps are always the same regardless of what bean you are making; only the cooking times change. Here are some guidelines, but overall just trust your tastes. The beans are done when at least 5 to 8 of them taste tender and cooked through. Keep simmering until you get there. Easy shit.

HOT TIP: Beans tend to triple in size when you cook them, so if you want to end up with about 1½ cups of cooked beans (the standard can measurement), you want to start with ½ cup dried beans.

First, pick through your dried beans and throw out any fucked-up-looking ones and then rinse the winners. Put them in a big container and cover them with a couple inches of water. They are going to swell up as they soak and you don't want those fuckers popping up out the water. Soak them overnight or for at least 4 hours. This helps you cut down on your cooking time. Just throw them in the water to soak before you go to work and then they are ready to cook when you get home. Simple shit.

When you are ready to cook the beans, drain the soaking water and add the beans to a soup pot. You can add some carrots, onions, celery, or bay leaves for flavor, but that shit is not required. Add a bunch of fresh water to the pot, enough to cover the beans by at least 3 inches. Simmer this pot, uncovered, until the beans are tender. Add a couple pinches of salt in the last 10 minutes of cooking to flavor the beans. Drain off any liquid. If you used any veggies, discard (or compost) them. Store the cooked beans in the fridge or freezer until you are ready for them. No can opener required.

Here are some general cooking times for beans, but that shit really does depend on how long you soaked your beans, how old they are, and how much you love them. Just pay a little bit of attention and this will all turn out just fine.

BEAN COOKING TIMES

Black beans: 1 to 1½ hours

Black-eyed peas: 1 hour

Cannellini beans: 1½ hours

Chickpeas (garbanzo beans, same shit): 1½ hours

Kidney beans: 1½ hours

White, Great Northern, and navy beans: 1 to 1½ hours

Pinto beans: 1½ to 2 hours

BEETS

Beets are the taproot of the whole beet plant, like carrots, meaning they grow underground like a top-secret veggie snack. This is why they are so dirty in the store when you're buying them fresh. And yeah, the greens are edible too and legit delicious. Beets are a member of the plant family Amaranthaceae. Its relatives are Swiss chard, spinach, and quinoa so unsurprisingly, all these guys taste fucking awesome together.

Red is obviously the iconic beet color, but they actually come in a variety of shades, including yellow, striped on the inside like a candy cane, and all white. A variety of beet known as the sugar beet is the source of around half of the world's refined sugar. Not too bad for an ugly root.

Beets are good sources of vitamins and minerals like manganese, potassium, iron, and vitamin C. They are also rich in folate and betaine. These nutrients work together to help lower blood levels of homocysteine, which inflames your arteries and increases your risk of heart disease. Yeah that's right, they keep your heart beeting. Had to do it. That classic red beet color is from betacyanin, a plant pigment that some preliminary research indicates might help defend cells against harmful carcinogens. But more important, it will straight up turn your pee and poo red to the point you might think you're dying until you remember you ate some fucking beets. Beets always get the last laugh.

Beets are harvested summer through late fall but store super well and can keep for months when kept cool. Store beets without their greens in an unsealed bag in your fridge. If you like beet greens or just happen to buy some with the greens still attached, cut 'em off and wrap them loosely in a damp paper towel and keep them in your crisper for about a week. You can cook them like you would most greens (see page 236). Raw beets can taste kinda earthy, but when you roast or grill them, all those sugars come out and they taste sweet and damn delicious. Think you hate beets? Roast them or just try our Beeteroni (page 200) and get back to us with an apology.

101 HOW TO ROAST BEETS

Preheat the oven to 400°F.

Slice all the leaves and shit off the top of the beets, scrub them clean, but leave the skin on. Try to grab beets of the same size so they all roast at the same speed. Wrap them all together in one large piece of foil, then stick those blood-red bastards in the oven. (Put them on a baking sheet in case they leak a little.) Roast them until you can stick a fork in them with no resistance, 45 minutes to 1 hour.

When the beets have chilled for a bit, hold one in a paper towel and use the paper towel to kinda rub the skin off. If you cooked those bitches long enough this should be easy. You can store them in the fridge for up to 1 week to throw into salads or grain bowls, or use them right now.

If you like to eat beets on the regular, then don't stress about roasting them all on their own all the damn time. Next time you're baking any savory dish at 375°F or higher for a while, just toss a foil packet of these fuckers in and let them bum a roast ride. Just keep an eye on them if the temperature is higher than 425°F because they can dry out. If that shit starts to happen, just add a tablespoon of water to the foil packet when you check on them.

BELL PEPPERS

While you can find bell peppers at almost any grocery store, they are low-key nutritional powerhouses. They have triple the vitamin C of an orange, which helps with immune health and fight against heart disease, and have more potassium than a banana. Potassium-rich foods such as bell peppers have been shown to help in lowering blood pressure and protecting against heart disease and strokes. Not too bad for a normcore produce section staple.

They are available year-round but like most peppers, bell peppers are at their peak in mid- to late summer. Green bell peppers are largely disgusting because they are the unripe version of their more colorful and better-tasting brethren. Grab a yellow, orange, red, or even purple one instead for a superior and sweeter taste. Once they make it home, store bell peppers in the crisper drawer of your fridge, where they will last 1 to 2 weeks. Just make sure they are dry when you pop them in. If not, they'll start getting soft and could mold, which is almost as fucking gross as a green bell pepper. Bought a ton but can't use them all? Roast them, blend them up with a little veggie broth or nondairy milk and oil, and freeze that sauce for a rainy day.

101 HOW TO ROAST BELL PEPPERS

Stop buying roasted peppers in a jar like an asshole. Just light your money on fire if you don't give a fuck. This shit is super easy to do and will save you money. Grab some foil and peppers, and get your ass to the stove. This method is perfect for big, sweeter peppers like bell peppers, poblanos, and large banana peppers.

Place each pepper on the burner of a gas stove and turn the heat to high. Burn the shit out of the skin of each pepper, rotating it until every side has blackened. This whole process will take about 8 minutes.

When the peppers are blackened all over, place each one in a piece of foil and wrap it up tight so that no steam can escape. Let them sit and cool for 15 minutes.

When the peppers have cooled, the burnt skin will feel a little separated from the flesh of the pepper and you should be able to peel that shit off no problem. Don't run the pepper under the tap thinking you are saving time. You will lose the awesome roasted flavor if you do that, so don't fuck things up now.

Once the peppers are cleaned, go make something badass. You can do this shit a day or two in advance, just keep them in the fridge. Blend them into sauces like our House Marinara (page 197) or dips like Roasted Bell Pepper and Rosemary Dip (page 75), or add them to some tamales (page 4) or pasta salad (page 109). Go fucking nuts.

BROCCOLI

Broccoli is a branched vegetable with green or purplish flower buds that make it look like little trees when you chop it up. Oh you didn't realize that when you eat broccoli that you're eating the flower buds and stalks? Yeah, that's some fancy shit you've def not been appreciating. You want those buds to look tight and fresh in color when you're buying it. If it's starting to look yellowish or isn't firm, don't fucking buy it. Broccoli belongs to the cruciferous family that shares its ancestry with other flowering plants, like cabbage, cauliflower, Brussels sprouts, and kale. And like all those, it can be eaten raw or cooked. Your call. Don't forget about the stem either. Shave the harder outside with a veggie peeler and then chop that fibrous fucker up like you would the rest of the broccoli. It tastes great and you already paid for that shit, so why waste it?

Broccoli is a good source of fiber and protein, and contains iron, potassium, calcium, selenium, and magnesium as well as the vitamins A, C, E, and K. Broccoli, like other cruciferous vegetables, helps protect the heart by reducing the damage to arteries that leads to hardening, which is often a precursor to a heart attack or stroke. Plus all the fiber will have you more regular than your mom's trip to Starbucks. Broccoli is basically a toothbrush for your colon, yummmmmmm. Broccoli doesn't really last more than 3 to 5 days when you get it home from the store. Wrap it in paper towels or in a ventilated bag to get the most mileage, but don't seal that shit. Trapped moisture will make it turn way faster, which is basically wasting your damn money. Can't eat it all before it goes bad? Chop it up, then steam it for 3 to 5 minutes, dunk it all in ice water to cool them off, let the broccoli dry a little, then stick them in the freezer in a bag. The broccoli should keep for about 6 months. Throw it into your next soup or stir-fry frozen and appreciate how you planned that shit out.

BRUSSELS SPROUTS

Brussels sprouts have come a hell of a long way in the past 20 years, from a boiled, depressing side dish to a high-end culinary staple and beloved veggie. Brussels sprouts are named after Brussels, Belgium, where it is believed they were first widely cultivated 500 years ago. They look like mini cabbages or little brains depending on which child you ask. And no, Brussels sprouts didn't suddenly get better tasting, we just learned how to cook them. Like kale, cabbage, and broccoli, Brussels sprouts are a cruciferous vegetable and have a sulfur-containing phytochemical called glucosinolate, which is responsible for their distinctive odor and bitter flavor. Overcooking them, particularly through boiling, will intensify these bitter flavors and odors. But when you cook them correctly they actually have nutty sweetness that you can't stop eating. So yeah, we did that shit to ourselves.

Brussels are rich in vitamin C, vitamin K, folate, fiber, and carotenoids like beta-carotene, lutein, and zeaxanthin, all of which promote eye health. In fact, one cup of cooked Brussels sprouts has more than 150 percent of the minimum daily vitamin C requirement and 250 percent of vitamin K. They are available throughout the year, but peak growing season is fall through early spring. If you're lucky, you can find them still on their stalk looking like some kind of medieval bat. These guys stay fresh way longer than when you buy them already chopped off. You want to buy sprouts that are bright green with tightly compacted leaves. Just like all cruciferous veggies, any yellow or wilted leaves are sign that these guys are old as fuck. Once you get them home, you want to keep them cool and dry in the fridge, where they'll last 1 to 2 weeks. You'll know they are past their prime when you start seeing black spots and they generally look gross. Before you cook them, slice off the bottom where they attached to the stalk and pull off any weird-looking outer leaves. And if you decide to boil them and then complain that they're gross, that shit is on you. Again.

Got some hanging around you can't eat all at once? Try pickling those fuckers (see page 195) for a longer fridge life. They are great in salads, as a random snack, and put out on a tray with dips, fresh veggies, and olives if you want to make a fancy but lazy dinner for yourself.

CABBAGE

While kale has gotten all the love lately, its normal-ass cousin cabbage is just as nutritious and usually way cheaper. Cabbage is part of the plant family Brassicaceae, which is full of kale, cauliflower, broccoli, mustard, radishes, and all kinds of other greens. So yeah, it's well connected. If the only time you eat cabbage is in mayo-heavy slaw, reexamine your life. Cabbages are huge, cheap, everywhere, and fucking delicious. Cabbage is that bitch that can do it all: sharp and crunchy when sliced raw in salads and slaws, soft and kinda buttery when braised, nutty and sweet when stir-fried, and still crispy even when fermented. Cabbage has fucking range so relegating it to a barbecue side dish is a goddamn shame.

Cabbage has your ass covered when it comes to health benefits too. It's packed with fiber and low in calories so you can eat a ton of it to get all that dietary fiber your body desperately needs. It's also full of vitamins A, C, and K, plus folate, potassium, and magnesium. It probably knows where aliens are. Cabbage is also packed with flavonoids called anthocyanins, which give certain cabbages their red-purple color. These phytonutrients protect against oxidative stress and chronic inflammation. And sure, it might make a lot of people fart, but considering all the other shit cabbage does for us that seems like a fair trade.

When picking them out at the store you want them to feel heavy for their size and for the leaves to be kinda compact without any black or mushy spots. One you get them home, though, cabbages will keep for a long time. Store them whole in your fridge and they'll keep for more than a week and a half, easy. Sure, you might have to pull off some of the outer leaves if they start to wilt, but no big deal. Once you start cutting it up, you've got 2 to 3 days before it's passed its prime. So stop only eating kale and get back with the brassica that started it all, cabbage.

CARROTS

Carrots are so common that it's easy to forget what a badass vegetable they are. They come in all kinds of colors and shapes but obviously long and orange is the classic. Before you even start, no baby carrots aren't really young carrots. They are ugly or weirdly shaped carrots that are shaved down to bite-size pieces so people will fucking eat them. Sure it cuts down on food waste because they aren't discarding them like they used to, but damn. Can't we all just agree that it's OK if all our fruits and vegetables aren't identical? Back to carrots. They are as versatile as they are common. They can be steamed, roasted, shredded, pureed, sautéed, eaten raw, pickled, and used in desserts. Yeah, you forgot about carrot cake for a sec, didn't you? And while most of us just eat the taproot, the leaves and stems are edible too. Throw these fuckers in a pesto or chop them up into a pasta salad and people will think you know what the fuck you're doing.

One single carrot contains more than 200 percent of your daily requirement for vitamin A, which comes from the beta-carotene that gives them their color. Carrots also provide a shit ton of fiber and some vitamins C, E, and K. So you should def show them more respect than kinda eating them when they appear at the bottom of a can of soup. Buy carrots that are firm, with no dark spots or mushy bits. They'll keep for 2 weeks or more in the fridge in a loose, kinda breathable bag. Just don't let them sit in a ton of water 'cause they just won't last. After reading this you are now legally required to always keep carrots in your fridge unless you are eating them ASAP because now you know better. Don't betray our fucking trust, okay?

CHILE PEPPERS

You can find some kind of pepper in almost every grocery store. The only thing that changes is the kinds based on where the hell you are in the world and what season it is. While bell peppers (see page 223) have a lot of the market locked down, there are two important other categories: sweet chile peppers and hot chile peppers. It's estimated that there are over 50,000 different kinds of chile peppers in the world so it's easier to just place them in the three big broad categories otherwise shit gets exhausting.

Speaking of complicated, if you're fucking confused between chilis, chiles, and peppers you aren't alone. So let's clear some shit up. Chili is a dish made with beans and spices. Chile with a capital C is a country, but also means fresh or dried peppers when it's lowercase. Peppers can mean the fruits of the plants in genus *Capsicum* in the nightshade family or berries from the plants in genus *Piper,* like black pepper. But from here on out we're talking chile peppers, which all originate from South America, mostly Peru and Bolivia. Why we all decided to use the same words to mean a billion different kinds of food and plants, we don't fucking know. But when we say peppers, we mean chile peppers from the genus *Capsicum*: jalapeño, bell, poblano, etc. We discussed bell peppers earlier; here are some other hall-of-famers worth knowing.

BIRD'S-EYE/THAI CHILE: This chile pepper has many names depending where you're eating it, but one thing stays consistent: these tiny fuckers are HOT. Bird's-eye chiles are commonly found in Southeast Asian cooking, and you can use them in our Fresh Chile Vinegar (page 211), which makes those tasty motherfuckers last so much longer than the fresh ones. They're the tiniest fresh pepper you'll find in the market at about ½-inch long and skinny, like a serrano. They'll all be piled together: red, green, kinda orange, whatever. No matter the color, they'll be hot. Store them in the fridge in a dry, ventilated bag otherwise they'll get soft and turn within a week.

CAYENNE: Yeah, that's right, cayenne is a real pepper and not just a fine red powder in your spice rack. The fresh chiles are skinny, elongated, and a bright red with moderate heat. But seeing a fresh cayenne is rare and usually occurs only in the warmer months when peppers are in season. So anytime you see us call for cayenne, we specifically mean the ground powder because we'd never make you crawl all over town for some exclusive pepper. We assume you've got a fucking life.

JALAPEÑO: The great jack-of-all-trades hot pepper. Kinda fat, green, and the length of your finger, you can find them fresh in most major grocery stores. Serve 'em chopped up over nachos, slip slices into your tacos and burritos, pickle them with some carrots (like we did in our first book), or sauté them with the onions in the base of your favorite soups and stews. They go with almost everything. Only downside is that you can never tell just how hot one is until you cut that fucker up. If the spice is too much for you, remove the seeds and membrane from the inside and use only the flesh of the pepper. This is an easy way to cut the heat without just leaving your jalapeños in the crisper to rot. Ready for a hot fact? Chipotle peppers aren't a different chile; they are just smoked jalapeños acting all fuckin' fancy.

SERRANO: Think of these as jalapeño's hotter and better-looking cousin. They're skinnier, a little longer, and consistently bring the heat that all jalapeños wish they had. They're about five times hotter, so know that if you're grabbing these fiery friends at the market you're in for a spicy night. It's a rookie mistake to mix up jalapeños and serranos at the store, but it's not a big deal if you do as long as you can hang with the heat. Otherwise, read the fucking signs. If you remember that they resemble what jalapeños would look like if they got into modeling, you shouldn't have any problems identifying them. Still too hot? Scrape out the seeds and membrane just like in jalapeños to cut some of the heat.

CITRUS

There's a bazillion different kinds of citrus out there. Some you can eat the skin, like kumquats, others have the thickest fucking rind you've ever seen, like a pomelo. Whatever you grab at the market know you're getting some vitamin C in the flesh and all kinds of fucking flavor in the skin. To get the flavors and essential oils out of the skin without the bitterness you gotta shred or finely mince that shit, which is called zest. Not sure how to zest? We got you.

HOW TO ZEST CITRUS

If a recipe calls for citrus zest, don't panic. Sometimes adding the juice will make things too watery or not flavorful enough, hence zest. Basically, you want to get all the flavorful essential oils from the outside layer of whatever citrus fruit you're using in the dish. There are two ways to do this shit:

METHOD 1: A GRATER

This is the easiest method, but more likely to fuck up your knuckles if you're not careful. Grab your box grater or if you have a finer grater you use for nutmeg or Parmesan, use that. Using the smallest holes of whatever grater you grabbed, gently scrape off the waxy outside colored layer of the citrus fruit. The white spongy layer (aka the "pith" if you want to get fucking technical) is bitter and gross like your ex, so don't grate down past that. Keep going around the outside of the fruit until you get enough for your recipe.

METHOD 2: A KNIFE/VEGGIE PEELER

This way requires a steady hand but we think you're ready. WE FUCKING BELIEVE IN YOU. Take your sharp knife or veggie peeler and shave off a thin-ass layer of the rind. Set that on your cutting board, cut it into crazy-thin strips, then dice those up so you get a sort of minced-up zest. With this method you get more of the oils to stay in the skin where you need it, instead of all over your grater, which is all any of us really wants in life.

CUCUMBERS

Are you one of those people who never drinks any water and wonders why the fuck your body is falling apart? Then the cucumber is your new best friend. Cucumbers are 95 percent water, so if you can't seem to muscle down a glass of the wet stuff start snacking on these crispy sons of bitches and get yourself hydrated. You'll also be getting minerals like copper, phosphorus, potassium, and magnesium, which your body needs to keep your organs working and you feeling fresh. Cucumbers are part of the plant family Cucurbitaceae, making them both a gourd and a fruit. Yeah that's right, they grow on vines and are more like a melon than celery. Nature is fucking bonkers.

Cucumbers should go straight into the fridge to keep them fresh and crisp. Cucumbers will last between 5 and 7 days in the fridge as long as excess water and humidity is kept to a minimum, so dry those fuckers before you put them away. They are great in salad, in cold pastas, to dip with instead of chips, and smashed up in a cocktail. Bought too many? Fucking pickle them (see page 195). Come on. Why the fuck do you think pickles were invented?

IF YOU ARE WHAT YOU EAT
MIGHT AS WELL EAT SOMETHING
FUCKING BEAUTIFUL

CALLING THEM PLANT-EGGS SOUNDS WAY WORSE

EGGPLANT

The eggplant has never been more popular thanks to horny people and cellphones, but y'all still get freaked out by this alien-looking motherfucker when it comes to buying it in the store. Eggplant is a member of the nightshade family, like tomatoes, potatoes, bell peppers, and jalapeños, so don't let its looks get to you. Sure, it's got weird smooth seal skin and comes in a bunch of colors and patterns, but inside? Some of the best flesh in the game. Yeah, we said it. Eggplant doesn't have big concentrations of any specific vitamin or mineral but it's got a big enough spread between its fiber, folate, phosphorus, magnesium, zinc, and calcium that's still worth eating. It's just out here doing its best.

Eggplant is at its peak from summer to early fall so buy it then because it will be its tastiest and cheapest self. When you're picking one out, it should be firm and heavy for its size, and its skin should be smooth and glossy. Does it feel kinda floppy and look sorta shriveled in some spots? Don't buy that old motherfucker. You can roast, stew, bake, or fry eggplants and they'll kinda take on the flavors of whatever you season them with, so always go big. Plus when you mush or puree the flesh, it gets so damn creamy that you won't ever want another kind of dip. If you are gonna eat the eggplant you bought in the next 2 days you can leave it out on the counter, otherwise throw that shit in the fridge in a breathable bag and it should last for a week.

FENNEL

You're probably thinking "what the fuck is fennel?" but don't worry, we've got a crash course for your simple ass. Fennel has a white bulb with green stalks and feathery leaves—it almost looks like there's celery growing off a white onion with dill on top. The entire plant, from the bulb to the leaves, seeds, and pollen, is edible and ALL that shit is healthy. Fennel seeds are frequently used in medicine for their antioxidant and anti-inflammatory effects. Fennel itself is also a solid digestive aid, especially for treating things like heartburn and bloating (that's that anti-inflammatory shit). Matter of fact, a lot of food manufacturers use fennel to flavor things like candy or soda because fennel has an anise-like flavor, like black licorice but not so gross. You might be thinking you have no fucking idea what fennel tastes like, but fennel seeds are one of the main flavors in most Italian sausages so you totally do.

Fennel is part of the plant family Apiaceae, like carrots, dill, and parsnips, which makes sense because all their fronds look similar and they all taste fucking delicious together. Fennel is full of vitamin C, potassium, and folate, all of which you need to keep an adult body running smoothly. The dietary fiber in fennel can help limit cholesterol buildup and, frankly, poo buildup. Nobody likes someone who is full of shit, so eat your fucking fennel. When you're buying fresh fennel, check the bottom to make sure the root isn't looking brown and dried out. You want it to feel firm and the fronds to look fresh. Throw it in your fridge when you get home in a loose bag and it will last 5 to 10 days, depending on how fresh it was when you got it. The bulb can be eaten raw (like dipped in hummus or folded into a salad), roasted, and sautéed into soups and sauces. Keep the fronds and use them at the end to make dressings, salads, and soups look fancy.

FIGS

Humans have been eating figs for as long as we can remember. These sweet little bundles of flavor are fucking delicious on their own and go with so many things, from rice to balsamic vinegar. The fig originated in northern Asia Minor and spread throughout Asia and, thanks to the Greeks and the Romans, throughout the Mediterranean. Spanish missionaries brought the fig to Southern California in the 1500s, leading to the variety known as the Mission fig, which is still the easiest fig to find in the U.S. But figs are way older than that. Sumerian stone tablets from 2500 B.C. talk about eating figs, and parts of a fig tree were found during excavations of Neolithic sites from 5000 B.C. So yeah, you are basically genetically predisposed to love figs.

While we all think of figs as a fruit *nerd alert* it's actually a syconium: a group of tiny flowers growing inside an edible shell. Yeah, it's some otherworldly shit. Figs are a good source of calcium, fiber, iron, and potassium and rich in natural sugars. They can be eaten whole, baked, fried, grilled, raw, or roasted. Yeah, they can do it all. Dried figs are common all over the world because the fruit is so delicate and doesn't last a long-ass time after you pick it. Figs

have two seasons: a quick, shorter season in early summer and a second main crop that starts in late summer and runs through fall. They hate the cold, so it's harder to find figs if you live in a climate that gets legit winters. Look for figs that are still plump but not soft and squishy. A split in them is fine as long as they are oozing juice all over the place. You are gonna want to eat them a day or two after getting them home because they just don't last. They come in a ton of different colors, with slightly different tastes, but they all look a little like a Hershey's Kiss mixed with a testicle. Get over it and try these weird, delicious, old-as-fuck dudes.

Can't find them fresh? Dried figs plump back up to an okay place after you soak them in some warm water for at least 30 minutes. This would work for our Figs in a Blanket (page 87) no problem.

GARLIC

Nothing compares with garlic. Humans all over the world have been eating garlic in one form or another for thousands of years because we fucking love it. Garlic is in the *Allium* genus along with onions, shallots, and leeks and it's related to lilies. It's native to Central Asia and northeastern Iran but it was too damn good not to share so garlic quickly spread all over the world.

Garlic grows underground in the form of a bulb, which is what you buy when you grab it fresh at the store. Covered in an inedible papery skin, the bulb, or head, is broken up into individual sections called cloves, which is what we call for in our recipes. DO NOT MIX UP BULBS/HEADS

WITH CLOVES. We love garlic but damn, adding a whole head of garlic to a recipe that called for a clove is a serious fuck-up.

Before adding fresh garlic to a recipe, you gotta take off the papery skin. We assume that you know this but better safe than fucking sorry. There are all kinds of weird, complicated hacks online showing you how to remove this, but don't overthink this shit. Just press down on a clove with the flat side of your knife until it kinda pops and then the skin should easily peel off. Done. Garlic contains a sulfur compound called *allicin* which is one of the components of the classic pungent garlic taste. The more you chop, grate, or mince garlic the more *allicin* is released and more garlicky your food will taste. So, only want a little garlic taste? Chop it. Want more garlic for your buck? Mince or grate it.

Fresh garlic will keep for weeks in a cool, dark, dry place. Don't ever buy that minced, jarred garlic shit. It's fucking terrible and barely tastes like the real thing. And while granulated garlic and garlic powder taste different than fresh, we still fucking love them and use them in a ton of recipes. Wanna take your love of garlic to the next level? Roast that shit.

101 HOW TO ROAST GARLIC

Roasted garlic adds a nice buttery sweetness to just about anything and it's easy as fuck to make at home. Restaurants that charge extra for roasted garlic should be fucking ashamed.

Crank the oven to 400°F.

Pull off all the extra layers of skin around the bulb of garlic. You want that son of a bitch to stay in one piece but it doesn't need all that skin holding it back. Chop the top ¼ inch off the bulb to expose the tops of the cloves. Wrap it up in foil and pour ½ teaspoon olive oil over the top, then close it up.

Roast this in the oven until all the cloves look all golden and smells goddamn delicious, about 40 minutes. Just be careful when you're opening the foil to check on it because, you know, it was just in the goddamn oven.

Let it cool for a bit and then squeeze out as many cloves as you need. It will keep for at least 2 weeks in the fridge.

GINGER

Ginger is in the plant family Zingiberaceae (rolls off the tongue, right?), which includes cardamom and turmeric. It's the rootstalk of the ginger plant, or the rhizome if you're nasty. Ginger contains a metric fuck ton of antioxidants, right up there with pomegranates. Since humans have been humaning, ginger has been prized for all it does for the stomach. It fights inflammation, combats motion and seasickness, and destroys farts on sight. Ginger tea has been around since the dawn of time, so next time you get a bellyache, chop up some ginger and throw it in a cup of water with a squeeze of lemon and something to sweeten it up. See? Our ancestors knew what the fuck was up.

You can find ginger in most grocery stores about a bazillion different ways.

Sure, you can pick up the fresh root in the produce department, but dig around the other aisles and you can find it pickled, crystallized, candied, and ground up. We like pickled for sushi and rice bowls, crystallized, candied, and ground for baking. Everything else needs that fresh shit. When you're picking it out make sure it's fresh-looking, firm, smooth, and free of mold, with no signs of decay or wrinkled skin. Lookin' wrinkly and dried out? That motherfucker is old and not worth your time. Fresh ginger can be stored in the fridge for 2 to 4 weeks. When cooking with it, you need to peel off the skin but you can do that shit by scraping it with a spoon. Easy. Bought a lot and don't wanna waste it? Scrape off the skin, then freeze the remaining root whole. Then you can just grate it right from the freezer into whatever dish you need it for. It will keep for at least 6 months in there.

GREENS

You're a fucking grown-up and you should be eating your fucking greens. Sure, you might have a side salad once in a while, which is great, but that's not nearly enough and not really the greens we are talkin' about. While lettuces are sweet, soft, and best eaten raw, cooking greens are tougher and can handle some heat. There are more than 1,000 dark leafy green varieties eaten all over the world so we're only gonna focus on the hits, from the tender greens like spinach, dandelion, bok choy to the studier chard, collards, and kale.

Whatever the fuck you're eating, all dark green leafy vegetables are healthy as hell

for you. They are rich in vitamins A, C, E, and K and full of carotenoids. They also contain a fuck ton of fiber, iron, magnesium, potassium, and calcium. Studies have shown that eating two to three servings of green leafy vegetables per week may lower the risk of stomach, breast, and skin cancer. So why aren't you eating these healthy sons of bitches all the damn time?

When grabbing them at the store, buy leaves that look fresh and aren't wilted or floppy. Store them wrapped in a paper towel in a loose plastic bag in the fridge and they should last about a week. Looking a little wilted? Throw the greens in some cool water for a couple of minutes, then rinse and let it sit. They should start to freshen back up. Wanna eat more greens but can't chomp down fast enough? Buy that shit in the frozen aisle and toss them into soups, pastas, and stir-fries whenever you are short on the fresh stuff.

GREEN BEANS

Maybe you grew up calling them string beans or snap peas, but no matter what the fuck you say they're always worth eating. But there is some variety out there when it comes to what you find in the store. Green beans are typically long, rounded, and predictably green. Back in the day they used to have a long, fibrous string down their sides (think celery) and parents all over the world made their kids destring those fuckers before cooking them until farmers bred this trait mostly out of the plants. There are yellow and purple versions out there typically labeled wax beans but their shape and flavor are almost identical to your typical green bean. And yeah, they can be cooked in exactly all the same ways. Haricots verts, or French green beans, are a smaller, more tender, and slightly sweeter type of green bean. These fucks are always way more expensive than regular green beans, but unless you are a real bean-head, they prob aren't worth the marked-up price. Green beans are in the same family as shell beans, such as pinto beans, black beans, and kidney beans. But unlike their fussier family members, the entire bean, pod and seed, can be eaten.

Green beans might be low in calories but these slender motherfuckers are dense in nutrients. They're a good source of vitamin C, fiber, folate, vitamin K, and silicon, which you need for healthy bones, skin, and hair. Fuck those weird gummy bears that are supposed to help your hair and skin shine; just eat some damn green beans. When buying your beans, look for ones that are smooth and bright in color and don't have lots of brown spots or bruises. They should have a firm texture and snap when broken, which you can def do in the produce department when you are buying them to see how fresh those green fucks are.

When you get them home, store them unwashed in a loosely sealed bag in your fridge. They'll keep for about a week this way. Whole beans should keep for about seven days. Gotta a hot deal on a ton but can't use them all? Steam them for 2 to 3 minutes, dunk them in ice water to cool them off, let them dry, and stick them in the freezer in a bag. They should keep for

about 6 months. Can't find them fresh? Grab them from the frozen aisle and they'll be great, but skip the canned version. Those fuckers are gross and reserved for eating on a dare only.

HERBS

Fresh herbs are the best way to add a shit ton of flavor to a meal while also making it seem fancy as fuck. We've broken down the top three we use in this book but just know, when in doubt, add fresh herbs. Particularly if your dish looks ugly as fuck. Sprinkle some basil or dill on top and BOOM, that shit looks gourmet.

BASIL: Even the biggest newbies in the kitchen know what the fuck basil is. The most common kind in the U.S. is Genovese, which is exactly what you think of when you think of pesto and pasta. Its sweet leaves have been all over for years, but there are more than 50 different kinds you've probably never fucking tasted. There's lemon basil, Thai basil, holy basil, cinnamon basil, even an African blue kind. Depending on where you live, Genovese is probably not the basil you think of when you think of basil. We all got our own. While they all taste and look so different, with red, purple, and blue leaves and round or pointed shape, they are all related. Basil is a member of the plant family Lamiaceae alongside other herbs we all love, like mint, rosemary, sage, and lavender. Humans have been cultivating basil for more than 5,000 years, which explains why there are a bazillion different kinds that have traveled all over the world. We love that shit so much we couldn't travel anywhere for thousands of years without taking it with us.

While we rarely eat big enough quantities of basil for its vitamin and mineral profile to matter, it's full of all kinds of flavonoids and volatile oils that are good for your health. Estragole, linalool, eugenol, and limonene all give basil its many unique flavors and help fight inflammation. All basils have delicate leaves so you wanna pick a bunch out that looks fresh and bright. Avoid leaves with dark spots or shriveled stems because that shit is old and not gonna last. Wrap it in a paper towel and put it in the fridge when you get it back from the store. If it's still got lots of stems attached, you can treat that shit like it's a bunch of flowers and stick it in a cup of water, put a loose plastic bag over the leaves, and throw it in the fridge to buy yourself a couple more days. Yeah they sell dried basil in the store, but aside from throwing it in some soups and sauces, we barely fucking use it. Nothing compares with fresh basil so stop trying. Got a bunch that's about to go bad? Make a pesto (see page 184), scoop it into an empty ice cube tray, and freeze that shit. When it's all frozen, transfer the cubes to a plastic bag for longer freezer storage. It's so nice when you think you've got nothing to eat to remember this shit in your freezer. Just toss the cubes in a warm pot with roasted veggies, pasta, rice, or beans and that sauce will warm up in no time and boom, there's your fucking dinner.

CILANTRO/CORIANDER: Ahhhhhh, cilantro. One of the most controversial herbs out there. You either love it or you love to hate it. Cilantro is the fresh leaves of the coriander plant, which is why many countries refer to the herb as fresh coriander leaves rather than cilantro. But don't be fooled, this is the same shit. It's part of the parsley family, which explains why so many people have trouble telling cilantro from flat-leaf parsley at the store. The leaves look very similar but cilantro tends to have rounder, more feathery leaves with multiple rounded points while flat-leaf parsley has more oblong leaves with sharper points. That sentence not helping you at all? Just break off a leaf and smell that fucker right in the produce aisle and that should clear up all the damn confusion. You can find coriander seeds and ground coriander in the spice aisle, but that tastes more like cumin than cilantro leaves despite being from the same plant. Cilantro is wild like that.

Speaking of wild, if you hate this herb it's probably not your fault. Fresh cilantro tastes bright, lemony, and kinda peppery unless you have a certain gene that makes this shit taste like soap. Y'all got a raw deal. It tastes all fucked up to these folks because they can detect the natural chemical aldehyde in the leaves where the rest of us can't. You have our pity if this is you. Know that. One half cup of cilantro has only 2 calories, provides 28 percent of your daily vitamin K needs, and is full of antioxidants. Basically, it means you no harm even if you fucking hate it.

Unlike a lot of herbs, the stems of cilantro taste just like the leaves, so don't waste your time trying to pull off the leaves to cook with. Just chop up the whole damn thing, stems and all. Add cilantro toward the end of whatever you're cooking because this fucker loses flavor fast with heat. When you get it home from the store, don't wash it until you're ready to use it 'cause the added moisture will only make that shit go bad faster. Store cilantro wrapped up in a paper towel in your crisper drawer or place the stems in a glass of water and cover the top loosely with a plastic bag in the fridge like a weird bouquet. It should keep for at least a week. Bought too much and it's gonna go bad? Make a pesto (see page 184) or Cilantro-Herb Sauce (page 88) and freeze it for when you need something fresh for dinner but you aren't about to leave your house.

DILL: Dill is more than just an herb used to flavor pickles, goddammit. While this feathery motherfucker is popular all over the world, particularly Eastern Europe and Russia, it still doesn't get enough love in the U.S. It's one of our favorite herbs and we basically never make a salad without throwing a fuck ton of fresh dill in there. Time for you to catch the hell up. Dill is in the plant family Apiaceae along with all your favs like carrots, celery, cumin, fennel, and parsley. Makes sense why you always see them hanging around together in soups now, huh? It's easy as fuck to grow, so even though it hates frost you can find it in the store year-round. You can find the seeds in the spice aisle too, but skip the dried dill herb unless it's an emergency. That shit is worthless when it comes to flavor. If that's all you've got and you're replacing it in a recipe that calls for fresh, expect to add more than the recipe is calling for because that flavor is muted as hell.

Dill is an excellent source of vitamins A and C, riboflavin, calcium, magnesium, folate, and manganese. Plus, it's been used forever to help soothe upset stomachs and reduce gas. Grab a bunch that is bright green, without any mushy or black-looking fronds. Store in the fridge wrapped in a paper towel and it should last you a couple of days. If you've got the room, place a bunch of dill in a jar or glass of water like it's a bunch of flowers, then cover the top loosely with a plastic bag and stick that shit in the fridge. That should last you at least a week. But true dill heads know that shit won't last a day because we're out here eating all of it.

JACKFRUIT

Jackfruit is having a goddamn moment. Fifteen years ago people in the U.S. had never heard of it and now it's on menus all over the country and in national grocery chains. Although it's a tropical fruit, you usually won't find this giant motherfucker in the produce section. In most cities, it's still way more common to find unripe jackfruit in a can rather than fresh in most cities. But holy shit, if you can find it fresh it's something to fucking see. Jackfruit is the largest fruit to come from a tree and it's massive. They can be 3 feet long and 2 feet wide and up to 120 pounds, although 10 to 50 pounds is normal. The outside is green and kinda feels like it should belong to a lizard 'cause it's covered in these green triangular bump things. Inside, the fruit is light colored and kinda stringy. Technically, what we eat is actually a giant, tough, fleshy flower and the light-colored seed-looking things on the inside are the fruit, but if you say that shit to someone they're def gonna call you a fucking nerd.

Jackfruit is in the plant family Moraceae which makes it closely related to figs and mulberries. When it is ripe it gets softer and sweeter, tasting almost like faint bananas or mangos. Unripe it has hardly any flavor, which makes it fucking perfect to cook with because it takes on whatever you put it in and gets a texture similar to pulled pork. When you're grabbing some from the store for any of our recipes, make sure you get unripe or young jackfruit canned in water, not syrup. That sweet shit is good but not for what we're doing in here. If you find it fresh, buy that shit and text some friends to split it with you because you're gonna have a ton. It's a great source of dietary fiber, vitamin C, and potassium but has very little protein, so don't start living off it only.

LEMONGRASS

Lemongrass is just what it sounds like. A long, hearty AF grass that kinda tastes like lemon with a bit of ginger. It's got a thick, rooty bottom where all the flavor is. It's used to flavor all kinds of shit, from soups to desserts. Fresh is always best, but if you have to, getting frozen is the next best option. If you see it dried, don't buy it. It's almost never worth it. Lemongrass is tough as hell to chew on so it's best thrown into shit while you're cooking in big chunks and kinda fished out later once it's flavored everything up. All over the world lemongrass is alleged to have all kinds of health benefits originating from the flavorful oil it puts out. It can be used as a diuretic and helps reduce inflammation. But mostly, it just makes everything it touches taste really fucking good.

You can find lemongrass in the produce section of well-stocked grocery stores near the herbs. If not, check a market that specializes in southern Asian ingredients if you're lucky enough to have one of those in your area. You don't? Fucking move. The stalks are about 1 foot long with a little longish bulb attached to the bottom. Sometimes you'll find lemongrass already cut up into 2- to 3-inch pieces and put in a little clamshell container. Get whatever the fuck you can find. Look for firm stalks that don't look dull or brown in any spots. Lemongrass stems can last 2 to 3 weeks in the fridge and can also be frozen for a couple of months.

Want to grow your own? If you buy some with the bulb still attached then you've basically got all you need for this shit. Stick it in a few inches of water on your countertop like it's a flower and let it soak until it starts to form some roots. Keep changing the water though, you fucking monster. This might take a few weeks so have some damn patience. Once the roots are over ½ inch long you can plant that fragrant motherfucker. It needs lots of sun so don't keep that shit in your dark-ass kitchen. If you do this right, you'll never have to pay for lemongrass again.

LETTUCE

When it comes to lettuce, there's so much more out there than just romaine and iceberg. *Lactuca sativa* is the broad category for all things lettuce in the plant family Asteraceae, which includes daisies (which is cool as fuck). But back to lettuce. There are just a few basic types: leaf lettuce, romaine, iceberg, and butterheads. While you can make a basic salad out of any of these leafy motherfuckers, their health benefits and best uses differ by type. Leaf lettuce, like the classic red and green leaf found on salad bars across the '90s, has a mild, sweet taste. You see versions of this lettuce picked young and sold as gem, baby, or in spring lettuce mixes. About 2 cups of your average leaf lettuce give you around 80 percent of your daily vitamin A, which is decent as fuck numbers for a side salad.

Romaine is the base of every Caesar salad and has the right amount of crunch to give even the most boring dressing something to hold on to. Sometimes you'll see romaine hearts in the store, but that's just regular romaine with the slightly tougher and bigger outer leaves pulled off. You'd think because you can find this shit everywhere it wouldn't have an impressive nutritional profile, but dammit, romaine delivers. Two cups of romaine lettuce provide roughly 30 percent of your daily requirement for folate, almost half your daily vitamin A, and almost all your vitamin K. Not bad at all. But then there's iceberg. Beloved for its crunch and cup-shaped leaves, iceberg lettuce has basically nothing to offer other than its water content. Use it for the crunch but don't expect any nutrition from this boring-ass lettuce. Last but not least is the fanciest green of the bunch: butterhead. These lettuces include Bibb, Butter, and Boston and are known for their soft leaves and sweet taste. Order a leafy salad at an upscale restaurant and 9 times outta 10 a butterhead is somewhere on that plate. They just feel fancy for some fucking reason. It helps that butterheads give you about 70 percent of your daily requirement of vitamin K and small amounts of iron and calcium. So basically you can't go wrong with any lettuce but iceberg.

When grabbing lettuce from the market, buy whole heads because while bagged lettuce is easy AF to use, it goes bad way faster. Pick out heads that have tightly packed leaves, are heavyish for their size, and are bright in color. Basically, does it look pretty fresh? Then buy it. Leave the heads intact and unwashed until you're ready to use because exposing them to water and cutting them up only make them spoil faster. Store them in the crisper drawer in your fridge with some paper towels or in a paper bag inside a breathable plastic bag. Whole heads should last 1 to 2 weeks. Looking a little wilted? Throw the head in some cool water for a couple of minutes, then rinse and let it sit. It should start to freshen back up. Just like when you water some flowers.

MUSHROOMS

There are a bazillion different kinds of mushrooms out there that we love to eat, but they all have one thing in common: They are a fungus that we want among us.

1 Cremini

2 Shiitake

3 Oyster

4 Yellow Oyster

5 Maitake

Grocery stores have started carrying way more varieties lately than just the classic white button mushroom, so we thought we'd break down some of our new favs that we use when we find them in the store.

CREMINI: This variety looks a lot like white button mushrooms, just brown on top. Creminis are baby portobello mushrooms, so you know they have a good, kinda meaty flavor and can be subbed in for button mushrooms when you want to take shit to the next level.

MAITAKE: These mushrooms are also called as hen-in-the-woods and they look like the fucking prom queens of the mushroom world. They have these brown, kinda overlapping leaf-looking things that make them as gorgeous as they are fucking delicious. They are sold in big clumps at the store, usually wrapped in plastic. Despite being on the larger side, these guys aren't chewy or spongy when cooked. Just kinda meaty and tender. Check them out in our Nashville Hot Shroom Sammie (page 110) and our Shroom Asada (page 128).

OYSTER MUSHROOMS: These are sold in clumps like maitakes at the store but are pale gray in color, with round caps and are way more fragile. They have a delicate seafood kind of flavor and soft texture, so they are good in stir-fries and sauces. If you live near a fancy grocery store or a stocked farmers market you can sometimes find them in different colors like a soft pink and bright yellow.

SHIITAKE: These mushrooms have a wide, thin light brown cap, whitish gills underneath, and a woody stem. You can find them as small a quarter to as big as your hand. The bigger these fuckers get the stronger their meaty, seafood-ish flavor is, so buy accordingly. When people talk about "umami" as a flavor and you're fucking lost, think of shiitake mushrooms because they are full of it. Because of their strong flavor they are great in soups and noodle dishes with lots of flavors like ginger and garlic.

No matter what kind of mushroom you use, you wanna look for unblemished mushrooms that aren't soggy or limp, with intact gills under their caps. When you get them home, store them in a paper bag or plastic bag with a paper towel in it in the crisper drawer of the fridge. Use them within a couple of days because mushrooms will get soft and sad fast in the fridge. Before you use them, just run them under water and brush off any dirt you see. People used to say you shouldn't get mushrooms wet because they'd absorb the water, but as long as you aren't soaking them in a fucking tub of water, you're fine.

OKRA

Okra is divisive, but if you hate it, it might be because you've only had shitty okra. When done right there's nothing better. While the leaves of the plant are edible, when people say "okra" they're always talking about the seed pod. You'll start seeing them around the store when the weather gets warm, and occasionally you find that shit in the freezer too. They look kinda like jalapeños but have flat edges instead of round. If you slice them up you see all their seeds, which are fucking delicious, and you'll notice that shit gets a little gooey and sticky. When sliced, okra releases mucilage that some people hate, but in the right hands that fibrous motherfucker is no big deal. It's a member of the plant family Malvaceae, so it's related to your forever favs like cotton, cocoa, and hibiscus.

But okra isn't just a weird-looking seedpod that huge parts of the world fucking love to eat. Okra has good amounts of potassium, vitamin B, vitamin C, folic acid, and calcium. Also, 1 cup of okra has about 2 grams of protein, which is low-key exciting because once you get the hang of cooking it, you'll be demolishing okra by the panful. When you're buying it, look for smallish pods, less than 4 inches long, particularly if you're gonna cook that shit whole. They get a little woody and tough the bigger they get. There are reddish and green versions of the pods, but they taste the fucking same and red goes away when you cook them so buy whatever you want. Just get ones that are bright in color and not sticky or soft. You can eat them raw, so feel free to try one or two before you buy them if you can't tell how fresh they are. Throw them in a breathable bag when you get home and the okra will last a couple of days in the fridge. Bought a ton and can't eat it all? Cut it up and freeze that shit. Throw it into stir-fries, stews, or into a little flour and pan-fry it up. You're welcome.

PARSNIPS

"WTF is a parsnip?" is as true today as ever. While these cream-colored carrot lookalikes have been around forever they still aren't super common on dinner tables in North America. It's a member of the plant family Apiaceae, which also includes carrots, dill, cumin, and parsley. They are sweet but kinda dry so don't think you're just gonna chomp on it like a fucking carrot. While you can eat them raw, cooking them brings out their sweetness, so why do it any other way?

Parsnips are a huge source of fiber and have folate, vitamin C, and vitamin E. They're at their best in the late fall and winter because they get sweeter when farmers pick them after a frost. You want to buy the ones 6 to 10 inches in length. Any longer and they get a woody core you'd have to chew on for hours. Make sure they aren't soft or overly bendy because then they're old and won't be worth eating. Keep them loosely wrapped up in the fridge and they'll last at least a week. Go ahead, try the carrot's pale-as-fuck cousin and grow your goddamn palate.

POMEGRANATES

Pomegranates look like edible gemstones, and their juice is delicious, but these beautiful sons of bitches have a lot more to offer. They've been by our side as a tasty treat since the very beginning of human culture. Pomegranates are believed to have been domesticated almost 7,000 years ago in Northern India before quickly spreading all over the Middle East, North Africa, and the Mediterranean. That means humans

MOTHER NATURE IS WILD
AND Y'ALL ARE EATING CHICKEN NUGGETS

were planting pomegranates 2,000 years before the first pyramid was built so show some damn respect.

Pomegranates are packed with vitamin C and potassium, but they're most well-known for all their antioxidants. There's evidence that pomegranates can help to prevent some forms of cancer and can reduce the levels of plaque in arteries. The seeds also contain about 20 percent of your daily recommended fiber, so if all you're doing is juicing, you're losing.

Pomegranates are a winter crop with a short harvest window, so when you see those motherfuckers at the market act fast. The best way to get at the only edible part, the seeds (or arils, if you want to be fucking fancy) is easy but takes a few steps, so listen up. First, you wanna put the trumpety-looking end facing up. Cut a shallow pentagon kind of shape about an inch down from the top with that trumpet end in the center. Give the top a little tug and that part should pop off like a hat. Cut down the sides of the exterior following where all the segments are and then you can pull the whole thing apart like you're pulling open a closed flower. Pull off any of the dry flesh still hanging out, but all the arils should be right there, easy as hell to snack on or juice.

Store your pomegranates in a cool, dry place and they'll be fine for at least 3 weeks, depending on when they were picked. If you want to just store the seeds, put them in an airtight container in the fridge and they should last about 2 weeks.

SUMMER SQUASH AND ZUCCHINI

WTF is a summer squash? Summer squash, like zucchini, has a thin, soft skin and soft edible seeds, whereas winter squash has a hard skin like acorn squash. Pattypan, crookneck, eight ball, and yellow squash, whateverthefuck you find in your market is good to sub in whenever we call for summer squash or zucchini. Come summer these squash fucks are everywhere and cheap as hell. Summer squash are in the *Cucurbita pepo* genus, just like cucumbers, melons, and gourds such as pumpkins.

Summer squash are full of potassium, zinc, and magnesium as well as tons of B vitamins. You can eat them raw, roasted, and sautéed, and even the blossoms are fucking delicious. They can grow to massive sizes, but small and medium-size summer squash just taste better. You want them brightly colored, not all cut up on the outside, and not shriveled up anywhere. They will stay fresh for 4 or 5 days if you store them in a loosely closed bag in the fridge. If you're grabbing some squash blossoms, look for bright flowers with no wilting. When you get them home, sprinkle them with some water, then wrap them in a paper towel, and throw them in the fridge. Cook these fucks ASAP because they won't last long.

Got more summer squash than you can handle? Slice it into thin strips and fold it into your pasta when it is just out of the pot. The heat will wilt the squash and it will mix in to everything without standing out. Or there's always zucchini bread, the classic zucchini storage system.

TOMATOES

The word "tomato" comes from the Nahuatl *tomatl* since they are native to the Americas. Cortez stole that shit from the Aztec empire and brought tomatoes to Europe in the 1500s. Yeah, that's right, before then the Spanish and Italians didn't have any fucking tomatoes. No marinara, no pan con tomate, nothing. In fact, tomatoes are a member of the nightshade family, so when they came to Europe people were scared to eat them thinking that shit was poisonous. But don't blame the tomato 'cause they stay delicious all these years later. Tomatoes are the major dietary source of the antioxidant lycopene, which has been linked to heart health. They are full up of vitamin C, potassium, folate, and vitamin K. Not bad for a fruit we all pretend is a vegetable.

Keep your tomatoes on your kitchen counter, uncovered and away from direct sunlight if you're fancy and have windows in there. This will let them keep ripening and thus improve their flavor. They can last up to a week out there. DON'T PUT YOUR TOMATOES IN THE FUCKING FRIDGE. Doing so makes their texture mealy and gross. If your tomatoes are already ripe, you can stick them in the fridge to extend their shelf life by a couple of days but it's honestly not worth it. Also, note that tomatoes are in season in the late spring and summer. Eating them outside this window of time means they were picked while still green, trucked in from a billion miles away, and just aren't gonna taste all that good. Save that shit for summer.

WINTER SQUASH

Even though we call them winter squash, the season of these varieties of squash and pumpkins run from late summer to midwinter. And yeah, there's a ton of fucking varieties, from acorn squash, butternut, spaghetti, delicata, kabocha, all the way to cinderella pumpkins. What all winter squash have in common are thick, tough, kinda waxy shells that protect the sweet flesh inside. All winter squash are rich in carotenoids and full of magnesium, potassium, vitamin C, fiber, and even some protein. Despite being sweet, they have a low glycemic index and contain polysaccharides, which help prevent blood sugar from rising. Tasty and full of healthy shit? These guys deserve better than just pie and lattes.

Their thick skin allows these fuckers to last up to 3 months in a dark, cool pantry. No matter what variety of winter squash or pumpkin you choose, always pick squash that feels heavy for its size and doesn't have any cuts into the skin. When chopping them up, use a sharp knife and a level cutting surface because if you're being a stupid fuck, you will cut yourself. Winter squash is great steamed, sautéed, and roasted. Not sure what to do? Try our winter squash tamales and taste the fucking possibilities. Bought a ton and are already pushing that 2- to 3-month time limit? Chop, skin, and steam them, then freeze in a plastic bag to throw into soups, chili, smoothies, or pies as needed. They'll last at least 6 months this way.

STOP BUYING HALLOWEEN DECOR
SO YOU CAN AFFORD TO HOARD SOME GOURDS

ICON INDEX

❄ FREEZER FRIENDLY

Apple Mormon Muffins, 23
Artichoke Brunch Bake, 30
Baked Eggplant Rice, 119
Blackberry Sage Oat Bars, 36
Blueberry-Thyme Marble Rolls, 27–28
Carrot and Rice Soup, 55
Chipotle Pumpkin Tamales, 124–26
Creamy Curried Parsnip Soup, 59
Everyday Pizza Dough, 198–99
Grapefruit Cake, 158
Green Curry Paste, 214
House Marinara, 197
Jackfruit Pupusas132–34
Orange Cinnamon Morning Rolls, 32–33
Pesto, 184–86
Pomegranate Cola Jackfruit, 120
Pumpkin Scones, 38
Smoky Cabbage and Tomato Stew, 48
Sweet Potato Coconut Soup, 62
Tomato Rice, 85

🌾 GLUTEN FREE

Agua Fresca, 159
Artichoke Brunch Bake, 30
Artichoke Buffalo Dip, 66
Arugula and Fennel Salad, 50
Baba Ganoush, 84
Baked Eggplant Rice, 119
Baked Leeks and Parsnips, 97
Blackberry Sage Oat Bars, 36
Blueberry-Thyme Marble Rolls, 27–28
Blueberry-Thyme Preserves, 190
Brussels Sprout Hash, 43
Buffalo Sauce, 210
Cashew Cheese Sauces, 213
Chile Roasted Broccoli, 67
Chipotle Pumpkin Tamales, 124–26
Coconut Green Curry, 137

Cowboy Scramble, 39
Curtido, 78
Everyday Vinaigrette, 209
Fasolakia, 73
Fig and Ginger Fizz Punch, 152
Fresh Chile Vinegar, 211
Fresh Peach Pudding, 166
Fried Capers, 58
Gincident Cocktail, 168
Ginger Simple Syrup, 153
Glazed Bok Choy, 74
Greek Dandelion Greens, 83
Green Curry Paste, 214
Grilled Nectarine Soba Noodles, 127
Homemade Horseradish, 215
Horseradish and Dill Dressing, 208
Hot Chile Oil, 212
House Marinara, 197
Jackfruit Pupusas, 132–34
Kiwi Colada, 167
Maple Kumquat Preserves, 40
Mezcal Meltdown, 161
Mulled Spiked Apple Cider, 149
Orange Peel Cauliflower, 107–08
Orangesicle Bars, 162
Passion Fruit Preserves, 191
Pestos, 184–86
Pineapple Fried Rice, 96
Pistachio Herb Rice, 91–92
Plum Salsa, 81
Pomegranate Cola Jackfruit, 120
Preserved Lemon Vinaigrette, 210
Preserved Lemons, 192–93
Quick Pickled Red Onions, 195
Refrigerator Dill Pickles, 196
Roasted Bell Pepper and Rosemary Dip, 75
Roasted Corn Salsa, 79
Roasted Japanese Sweet Potatoes, 88
Sesame Vinaigrette, 206
Shaved Asparagus and Chive Salad, 47
Shredded Daikon Salad, 54
Shroom Asada, 128–29

Smashed Cucumber Salad, 53
Southwestern Slaw, 51
Strawberry Rosewater Cheesecake, 150–51
Swiss Chard Puttanesca, 68–69
Summertime Carrot Salad, 77
Teriyaki Jackfruit, 118
Tomato Rice, 85
Toulatos-Style Stuffed Tomatoes or Bell Peppers, 142–43
Whatever Grain Porridge, 37
Wine-Braised Artichokes, 70

♻ GOOD FOR LEFTOVERS

All-Seasons Tempeh Crumble, 203
Baba Ganoush, 84
Baked Eggplant Rice, 119
Basil Pesto Summer Pasta Salad, 109
Buckwheat Persimmon Pancakes, 35
Buffalo Sauce, 210
Carrot and Rice Soup, 55
Cashew Cheese Sauces, 213
Chipotle Pumpkin Tamales, 124–26
Coconut Green Curry, 137
Coconut Milk Whipped Cream, 189
Cowboy Scramble, 39
Creamy Curried Parsnip Soup, 59
Everyday Pizza Dough, 198–99
Everyday Vinaigrette, 209
Fasolakia, 73
Fresh Chile Vinegar, 211
Grapefruit Cake, 158
Green Curry Paste, 214
Green Grape Pie, 155–56
Grilled Nectarine Soba Noodles, 127
Horseradish and Dill Dressing, 208
Hot Chile Oil, 212
House Marinara, 197

Jackfruit Pupusas, 132–34
Lemongrass Baked Tofu, 122–23
Mulled Spiked Apple Cider, 149
Orangesicle Bars, 162
Pantry Parm, 199
Pear and Pecan Pie, 170–71
Pear, Tempeh, and Arugula Sandwich, 100
Pineapple Fried Rice, 96
Pistachio Herb Rice, 91–92
Plum-Side-Down Cake, 165
Pomegranate Cola Jackfruit, 120
Preserved Lemon Vinaigrette, 210
Roasted Corn Salsa, 79
Roasted Japanese Sweet Potatoes, 88
Sesame Vinaigrette, 206
Shroom Asada, 128–29
Simple Sesame Noodles, 144–45
Smoky Cabbage and Tomato Stew, 48
Smoky Tempeh Slices, 204
Sticky Tofu, 135
Strawberry Rosewater Cheesecake, 150–51
Sweet Potato Coconut Soup, 62
Tomatillo and Cucumber Gazpacho, 61
Tomato Rice, 85
Toulatos-Style Stuffed Tomatoes or Bell Peppers, 142–43
Whatever Grain Porridge, 37
Winter Squash Blondies, 172
Zucchini Blossom Pasta, 140

LONGER COOKING TIMES, DINNER PARTY FAVS

Artichoke Buffalo Dip, 66
Baked Eggplant Rice, 119
Beeteroni Pizza, 104
Blueberry-Thyme Marble Rolls, 27–28
Caramelized Fennel Tarts, 113
Chipotle Pumpkin Tamales, 124–26
Coconut Green Curry, 137
Everyday Pizza Dough, 198–99
Fasolakia, 73
Figs in a Blanket, 87
Grapefruit Cake, 158

Green Grape Pie, 155–56
Jackfruit Pupusas, 132–33
Mulled Spiked Apple Cider, 149
Nashville Hot Shroom Sammie, 110–112
Orange Cinnamon Morning Rolls, 32–33
Orange Peel Cauliflower, 107–8
Orangesicle Bars, 162
Pear and Pecan Pie, 170–71
Pistachio Herb Rice, 91–92
Plum-Side-Down Cake, 165
Pomegranate Cola Jackfruit, 120
Romaine Hearts Salad, 56
Shroom Asada, 128–29
Strawberry Rosewater Cheesecake, 150–51
Summer Tomato Tart, 139
Teriyaki Jackfruit, 117–18
Toulatos-Style Stuffed Tomatoes or Bell Peppers, 142–43
Wine-Braised Artichokes, 70
Winter Squash Blondies, 172
Zucchini Blossom Pasta, 140
Zucchini Bundt Cake, 173

PANTRY STAPLES

All-Seasons Tempeh Crumble, 203
Baked Eggplant Rice, 119
Banana Date Shake, 148
Buffalo Sauce, 210
Cashew Cheese Sauces, 213
Coconut Milk Whipped Cream, 189
Everyday Vinaigrette, 209
Fried Capers, 58
Hot Chile Oil, 212
Horseradish and Dill Dressing, 208
House Marinara, 197
Mulled Spiked Apple Cider, 149
Pantry Parm, 199
Peanut Better Cookies, 175
Pineapple Fried Rice, 96
Preserved Lemon Vinaigrette, 210
Preserved Lemons, 192–93
Quick Pickled Red Onions, 195
Sesame Vinaigrette, 206
Simple Sesame Noodles, 144–45
Tomato Rice, 85
Winter Squash Blondies, 172

WEEKNIGHT GO-TOS, ONE-POT MEALS

Artichoke Brunch Bake, 30
Baked Eggplant Rice, 119
Basil Pesto Summer Pasta Salad, 109
Breakfast Spaghetti, 24
Broccoli Rabe Pasta, 103
Carrot and Rice Soup, 55
Coconut Green Curry, 137
Cowboy Scramble, 39
Creamy Curried Parsnip Soup, 59
Fasolakia, 73
Greek Dandelion Greens, 83
Jackfruit Pupusas, 132–34
Oklahoma-Style Fried Okra, 93
Pan Seared Okra, 95
Pineapple Fried Rice, 96
Pistachio Herb Rice, 91–92
Pomegranate Cola Jackfruit, 120
Simple Sesame Noodles, 144–45
Smoky Cabbage and Tomato Stew, 48
Stovetop Creamed Collards, 82
Sweet Potato Coconut Soup, 62
Tomato Rice, 85
Whatever Grain Porridge, 37

RECIPE INDEX

A

Agua Fresca, 159
Almonds
    Basic Herb Pesto, 184
    Horseradish and Dill Dressing, 208
    Pantry Parm, 199
    Shaved Asparagus and Chive
      Salad, 47
    Sun-Dried Tomato Pesto, 185
    Wilted Greens Pesto, 186
Apples
    Apple Mormon Muffins, 23
    Mulled Spiked Apple Cider, 149
Artichokes, 217, 219
    Artichoke Brunch Bake, 30
    Artichoke Buffalo Dip, 66
    Wine-Braised Artichokes, 70
Arugula, 217
    Arugula and Fennel Salad, 50
    Pear, Tempeh, and Arugula
      Sandwich, 100
Asada, Shroom, 128–29
Asparagus, Shaved, and Chive
    Salad, 47
Avocados, 220
    Coconut Green Curry, 137
    Plum Salsa, 81
    Romaine Hearts Salad, 56
    Southwestern Slaw, 51
    Summertime Carrot Salad, 77

B

Baba Ganoush, 84
Bananas, 220–21
    Banana Date Shake, 148
    Zucchini Bundt Cake, 173
Barley, 178
Bars
    Blackberry Sage Oat Bars, 36
    Orangesicle Bars, 162
Basil, 237–38
    Basic Herb Pesto, 184
    Basil Pesto Summer Pasta
      Salad, 109
    Green Curry Paste, 214
Beans, 221, 236–37
    Fasolakia (Greek Green
      Beans), 73
    Jackfruit Pupusas, 132–34

Roasted Bell Pepper and
    Rosemary Dip, 75
Sweet Potato Coconut Soup,
    62
Toulatos-Style Stuffed
    Tomatoes or Bell Peppers,
    142–43
Beets, 222
    Beeteroni, 200
    Beeteroni Pizza, 104
Blackberry Sage Oat Bars, 36
Blondies, Winter Squash, 172
Blueberry-Thyme Marble Rolls,
    27–28
Blueberry-Thyme Preserves, 190
Bok choy
    Coconut Green Curry, 137
    Glazed Bok Choy, 74, 106
    Teriyaki Jackfruit, 117–18
Bragg liquid aminos, 180
Breads
    Apple Mormon Muffins, 23
    Blueberry-Thyme Marble Rolls,
      27–28
    Homemade Old Bay Croutons,
      57, 187
    Orange Cinnamon Morning
      Rolls, 32–33
Broccoli, 224
    Broccoli Rabe Pasta, 103
    Chile-Roasted Broccoli, 67
Brussels sprouts, 2`24–25
    Brussels Sprout Hash, 43
Buckwheat Persimmon Pancakes,
    35
Buffalo Sauce, 210

C

Cabbage, 225
    Curtido, 78
    Smoky Cabbage and Tomato
      Stew, 48
    Southwestern Slaw, 51
Cakes
    Grapefruit Cake, 158
    Plum-Side-Down Cake, 165
    Zucchini Bundt Cake, 173
Capers
    Fried Capers, 58

Swiss Chard Puttanesca,
    68–69
Carrots, 226
    Carrot and Rice Soup, 55
    Curtido, 78
    Summertime Carrot Salad, 77
Cashews
    Cashew Cheese Sauces, 213
    Strawberry Rosewater
      Cheesecake, 150–51
Cauliflower, Orange Peel, 107–8
Cheesecake, Strawberry
    Rosewater, 150–51
Chickpea flour
    Artichoke Brunch Bake, 30
Chiles, 226–28
    Chile-Roasted Broccoli, 67
    Chipotle Pumpkin Tamales,
      124–26
    Fresh Chile Vinegar, 211
    Green Curry Paste, 214
    Hot Chile Oil, 212
    Mezcal Meltdown, 161
    Sun-Dried Tomato Pesto, 185
Chipotle Pumpkin Tamales, 124–26
Chives and Shaved Asparagus
    Salad, 47
Chocolate, melting, 180
Cilantro, 238–39
    Basic Herb Pesto, 184
    Green Curry Paste, 214
    Plum Salsa, 81
    Roasted Japanese Sweet
      Potatoes, 88
    Shroom Asada, 128–29
    Summertime Carrot Salad, 77
Cinnamon Orange Morning Rolls,
    32–33
Citrus, 228–29
Coconut
    Coconut Green Curry, 137
    Coconut Milk Whipped Cream,
      189
    Kiwi Colada, 167
    Orangesicle Bars, 162
    Strawberry Rosewater
      Cheesecake, 150–51
    Sweet Potato Coconut Soup,
      82

Collards, Creamed, Stovetop, 82
Cookies, Peanut Better, 175
Corn
    Basil Pesto Summer Pasta Salad, 109
    Roasted Corn Salsa, 79, 80
    Southwestern Slaw, 51
Couscous, 178
Cowboy Scramble, 39
Croutons, Homemade Old Bay, 57, 187
Cucumbers, 229
    Basil Pesto Summer Pasta Salad, 109
    The Gincident Cocktail, 168
    Refrigerator Dill Pickles, 196
    Roasted Corn Salsa, 79, 80
    Romaine Hearts Salad, 56
    Smashed Cucumber Salad, 53
    Tomatillo and Cucumber Gazpacho, 61
Curry
    Coconut Green Curry, 137
    Creamy Curried Parsnip Soup, 59
    Green Curry Paste, 214
    Teriyaki Jackfruit with Curry Udon Noodles, 117–18
Curtido, 78

D

Daikon, Shredded, Salad, 52, 54
Dandelion Greens, Greek, 83
Date Banana Shake, 148
Desserts
    Fresh Peach Pudding, 166
    Green Grape Pie, 155–56
    Orangesicle Bars, 162
    Peanut Better Cookies, 175
    Pecan and Pear Pie, 170–71
    Plum-Side-Down Cake, 165
    Strawberry Rosewater Cheesecake, 150–51
    Winter Squash Blondies, 172
    Zucchini Bundt Cake, 173
Dill, 239
    Horseradish and Dill Dressing, 57, 208
    Refrigerator Dill Pickles, 196

Dips
    Artichoke Buffalo Dip, 66
    Baba Ganoush, 84
    Roasted Bell Pepper and Rosemary Dip, 75
Dressing, Horseradish and Dill, 57, 208

E

Edamame and Watercress, Simple Sesame Noodles with, 144–45
Eggplant, 233
    Baba Ganoush, 84
    Baked Eggplant Rice, 72, 119

F

Fasolakia (Greek Green Beans), 73
Fennel, 233–34
    Arugula and Fennel Salad, 50
    Caramelized Fennel Tarts, 113
Figs, 234
    Fig and Ginger Fizz Punch, 152
    Figs in a Blanket, 87

G

Garlic, 234–35
    Glazed Bok Choy with, 74, 106
Gazpacho, Tomatillo and Cucumber, 61
Gincident Cocktail, 168
Ginger, 235–36
    Fig and Ginger Fizz Punch, 152
    Ginger Simple Syrup, 153
    Ginger-Turmeric Tofu Marinade, 123
    Sweet Potato Coconut Soup, 62
    Winter Squash Blondies, 172
Grains, 178–79
    Whatever Grain Porridge, 37
Grape, Green, Pie, 155–56
Grapefruit Cake, 158
Green beans, 236–37
    Fasolakia, 73
Green Curry Paste, 214
Greens
    Greek Dandelion Greens, 83
    Shaved Asparagus and Chive Salad, 47
    Wilted Greens Pesto, 186

H

Hash, Brussels Sprout, 43
Herbs, 237–39
    Basic Herb Pesto, 184
    Pistachio Herb Rice, 91–92
    Roasted Japanese Sweet Potatoes, 88
    Wilted Greens Pesto, 186
    Wine-Braised Artichokes, 70
    Horseradish and Dill Dressing, 57, 208
    Horseradish, Homemade, 215
Hot Chile Oil, 212

J

Jackfruit, 239–40
    Pomegranate Cola, 90, 120
    Pupusas, 132–34
    Teriyaki, 117–18

K

Kale
    Carrot and Rice Soup, 55
    Sweet Potato Coconut Soup, 62
Kiwi Colada, 167
Kumquat Preserves, Maple, 40

L

Leeks and Parsnips, Baked, 97
Lemongrass, 240
    Green Curry Paste, 214
    Lemongrass Baked Tofu, 122–23
Lemons
    Arugula and Fennel Salad, 50
    Preserved Lemons, 192–93
    Preserved Lemon Vinaigrette, 210
Lettuce, 241
Limes
    Pan-Seared Okra, 95
    Shroom Asada, 128–29
Liquid smoke, 180

M

Maple syrup
    Maple Kumquat Preserves, 40
    Peanut Better Cookies, 175
Marinade, Ginger-Turmeric Tofu, 123
Marinara, House, 197
Masa harina, 181
    Chipotle Pumpkin Tamales, 124–26
    Jackfruit Pupusas, 132–34

Mezcal Meltdown, 161
Millet, 178
      Whatever Grain Porridge, 37
Muffins, Apple Mormon, 23
Mulled Spiked Apple Cider, 149
Mushrooms, 241–43
      Nashville Hot Shroom Sammie,
         110–12
      Shroom Asada, 128–29

N
Nectarine, Grilled, Soba Noodles,
   127
Noodles
      Grilled Nectarine Soba
         Noodles, 127
      Simple Sesame Noodles,
         144–45
      Teriyaki Jackfruit, 117–18
Nut butters
      The Easier but Not as
         Delicious Nut Milk, 21
      Horseradish and Dill Dressing,
         57, 208
      Peanut Better Cookies, 175
Nut milks
      The Best Nut Milk, 20
      The Easier but Not as
         Delicious Nut Milk, 21
Nutritional yeast (nooch), 181
      Breakfast Spaghetti, 24
      Cashew Cheese Sauces, 213
      Cowboy Scramble, 39
      Pantry Parm, 199
      See also Pestos
Nuts, 46

O
Oats
      Blackberry Sage Oat Bars, 36
      Orangesicle Bars, 162
      Whatever Grain Porridge, 37
Oils, 183
      Hot Chile Oil, 212
Okra, 243–44
      Oklahoma-Style Fried, 93
      Pan-Seared, 95
Old Bay Croutons, Homemade, 57,
   187
Onions, Red, Quick-Pickled, 57, 195
Oranges
      Orange Cinnamon Morning
         Rolls, 32–33
      Orange Peel Cauliflower, 107–8

Orangesicle Bars, 162
Shroom Asada, 128–29

P
Pancakes, Buckwheat Persimmon,
   35
Panko bread crumbs, 181
      Broccoli Rabe Pasta, 103
      Panko Pasta Topping, 205
Pantry Parm, 199
Pantry staples, 182
Parm, Pantry, 199
Parsnips, 244
      Baked Leeks and Parsnips,
         97
      Creamy Curried Parsnip Soup,
         59
Passion fruit
      Preserves, 191
      Strawberry Rosewater
         Cheesecake, 150–51
Pasta
      Basil Pesto Summer Pasta
         Salad, 109
      Breakfast Spaghetti, 24
      Broccoli Rabe Pasta, 103
      Panko Pasta Topping, 205
      Smoky Cabbage and Tomato
         Stew, 48
      Zucchini Blossom Pasta,
         140
Paste, Green Curry, 214
Peach, Fresh, Pudding, 166
Peanut Better Cookies, 175
Pears
      Pear, Tempeh, and Arugula
         Sandwich, 100
      Pecan and Pear Pie, 170–71
Pecan and Pear Pie, 170–71
Peppers, 223. See also Chiles
      Cowboy Scramble, 39
      Roasted Bell Pepper and
         Rosemary Dip, 75
      Summertime Carrot Salad, 77
      Tomatillo and Cucumber
         Gazpacho, 61
      Toulatos-Style Stuffed Bell
         Peppers, 142–43
Persimmon Buckwheat Pancakes,
   35
Pestos
      Basic Herb Pesto, 184
      Basil Pesto Summer Pasta
         Salad, 109

Sun-Dried Tomato Pesto, 185
Wilted Greens Pesto, 186
Pickles
      Quick-Pickled Red Onions, 57,
         195
      Refrigerator Dill Pickles, 196
Pie Crust, Flaky, 188
Pies
      Green Grape Pie, 155–56
      Pecan and Pear Pie, 170–71
Pineapple
      Kiwi Colada, 167
      Mezcal Meltdown, 161
      Pineapple Fried Rice, 96
Pistachio Herb Rice, 91–92
Pizza, Beeteroni, 104
Pizza Dough, Everyday, 198–99
      Plum Salsa, 81
      Plum-Side-Down Cake, 165
Pomegranate, 244–46
      Pomegranate Cola Jackfruit,
         90, 120
Porridge, Whatever Grain, 37
Potatoes. See also Sweet
      potatoes
      Cowboy Scramble, 39
      Fasolakia, 73
Preserved Lemons, 192–93
Preserved Lemon Vinaigrette,
   210
Preserves
      Blueberry-Thyme, 190
      Maple Kumquat, 40
      Passion Fruit, 191
Pudding, Fresh Peach, 166
Pumpkin
      Chipotle Pumpkin Tamales,
         124–26
      Pumpkin Scones, 38
Punch, Fig and Ginger Fizz, 152
Pupusas, Jackfruit, 132–34

Q
Quinoa, 179
      Whatever Grain Porridge, 37

R
Rice
      Baked Eggplant Rice, 72, 119
      Basic Pot of Brown Rice, 179
      Carrot and Rice Soup, 55
      Pineapple Fried Rice, 96
      Pistachio Herb Rice, 91–92
      Tomato Rice, 85

Toulatos-Style Stuffed Tomatoes or Bell Peppers, 142–43
Whatever Grain Porridge, 37

Rolls
Blueberry-Thyme Marble Rolls, 27–28
Orange Cinnamon Morning Rolls, 32–33

Rosemary and Roasted Bell Pepper Dip, 75
Rosewater Strawberry Cheesecake, 150–51

S

Salads
Arugula and Fennel Salad, 50
Basil Pesto Summer Pasta Salad, 109
Romaine Hearts Salad, 56
Shaved Asparagus and Chive Salad, 47
Shredded Daikon Salad, 52, 54
Smashed Cucumber Salad, 53
Summertime Carrot Salad, 77

Salsa
Plum Salsa, 81
Roasted Corn Salsa, 79, 80

Sandwiches
Nashville Hot Shroom Sammie, 110–12
Pear, Tempeh, and Arugula Sandwich, 100

Sauces
Buffalo Sauce, 210
Cashew Cheese Sauces, 213
Cilantro-Herb Sauce, 88
House Marinara, 197

Scones, Pumpkin, 38
Seeds, toasting, 46
Sesame Vinaigrette, 206
Shakes, Banana Date, 148
Simple Syrup, Ginger, 153

Slaw
Curtido, 78
Southwestern, 51

Soups
Carrot and Rice, 55
Creamy Curried Parsnip, 59
Smoky Cabbage and Tomato Stew, 48
Sweet Potato Coconut, 62
Tomatillo and Cucumber Gazpacho, 61

Spaghetti, Breakfast, 24

Spinach
Pineapple Fried Rice, 96
Teriyaki Jackfruit, 117–18

Squash, 246, 247
Chipotle Pumpkin Tamales, 124–26
Pumpkin Scones, 38
Winter Squash Blondies, 172

Stew, Smoky Cabbage and Tomato, 48
Sticky Tofu, 94, 135–36
Strawberry Rosewater Cheesecake, 150–51
Sunflower Seeds, Basil Pesto Summer Pasta Salad with, 109

Sweet potatoes
Roasted Japanese Sweet Potatoes, 88
Sweet Potato Coconut Soup, 62

Swiss Chard Puttanesca, 68–69

T

Tahini
Baba Ganoush, 84
Horseradish and Dill Dressing, 57, 208

Tamales, Chipotle Pumpkin, 124–26

Tarts
Caramelized Fennel, 113
Summer Tomato, 139

Tempeh, 181
All-Seasons Tempeh Crumble, 203
Pear, Tempeh, and Arugula Sandwich, 100
Smoky Tempeh Slices, 204

Teriyaki Jackfruit, 117–18

Tofu, 121, 181
Artichoke Buffalo Dip, 66
Breakfast Spaghetti, 24
Coconut Green Curry, 137
Cowboy Scramble, 39
Ginger-Turmeric Tofu Marinade, 123
Lemongrass Baked Tofu, 122–23
Sticky Tofu, 94, 135–36

Tomatillo and Cucumber Gazpacho, 61

Tomatoes, 247
Baked Eggplant Rice, 72, 119

Basil Pesto Summer Pasta Salad, 109
Breakfast Spaghetti, 24
House Marinara, 197
Roasted Corn Salsa, 79, 80
Smoky Cabbage and Tomato Stew, 48
Summer Tomato Tart, 139
Sun-Dried Tomato Pesto, 185
Swiss Chard Puttanesca, 68–69
Tomatillo and Cucumber Gazpacho, 61
Tomato Rice, 85
Toulatos-Style Stuffed Tomatoes, 142–43
Zucchini Blossom Pasta, 140

Tortellini, Smoky Cabbage and Tomato Stew with, 48
Toulatos-Style Stuffed Tomatoes or Bell Peppers, 142–43
Turmeric-Ginger Tofu Marinade, 123

V

Vinaigrette
Everyday, 209
Preserved Lemon, 210
Sesame, 206

Vinegar, Fresh Chile, 211

W

Walnuts
Green Grape Pie, 155–56
Winter Squash Blondies, 172
Zucchini Bundt Cake, 173

Watercress and Edamame, Simple Sesame Noodles with, 144–45
Whipped Cream, Coconut Milk, 189
Wine-Braised Artichokes, 70

Z

Zucchini, 246
Breakfast Spaghetti, 24
Zucchini Blossom Pasta, 140
Zucchini Bundt Cake, 173

To our readers for their insatiable appetite.
Nick Hensley for breathing life into our ideas.
Kara Plikaitis for being a port in every storm.
Dervla Kelly for making sense of our nonsense.
Sally James for fighting for us since day one.
Richard Pine and Kim Witherspoon for the
steady hands. Saul Cooperstein for the vino and
advice. Ian Markiewicz and Megan Johnson for
being the chillest neighbors. Ron Finley for the
love. Ravi Malhotra for the laughs. Maya
Trammell for bringing the heat. Lauren Gamboa
and Lily Huber for the downtime. Roxy Storm
and Mick Weldon for their friendship and
penmanship. Alexis Linkletter for her relentless
support. Aaron Wehner, Marysarah Quinn,
Diana Baroni, Mark McCauslin, Tammy Blake,
Kelli Tokos, Christina Foxley, Brianne Sperber,
and the entire team at Penguin Random House
for lighting the path.

Last but not least, thanks to everyone who's
been with us from the beginning. Your support
over the years has meant more to us than we
could ever put into words. So we put it into food.

Michelle Davis + Matt Holloway